# The Salamanca School

**Series Introduction**

The *Major Conservative and Libertarian Thinkers* series aims to show that there is a rigorous, scholarly tradition of social and political thought that may be broadly described as 'conservative', 'libertarian' or some combination of the two.

The series aims to show that conservatism is not simply a reaction against contemporary events, nor a privileging of intuitive thought over deductive reasoning; libertarianism is not simply an apology for unfettered capitalism or an attempt to justify a misguided atomistic concept of the individual. Rather, the thinkers in this series have developed coherent intellectual positions that are grounded in empirical reality and also founded upon serious philosophical reflection on the relationship between the individual and society, how the social institutions necessary for a free society are to be established and maintained, and the implications of the limits to human knowledge and certainty.

Each volume in the series presents a thinker's ideas in an accessible and cogent manner to provide an indispensable work for both students with varying degrees of familiarity with the topic as well as more advanced scholars.

The following twenty volumes that make up the entire *Major Conservative and Libertarian Thinkers* series are written by international scholars and experts.

*The Salamanca School* by Andre Azevedo Alves (LSE, UK) &
 Professor José Manuel Moreira (Porto, Portugal)
*Thomas Hobbes* by Dr R. E. R. Bunce (Cambridge, UK)
*John Locke* by Professor Eric Mack (Tulane, US)
*David Hume* by Professor Christopher J. Berry (Glasgow, UK)
*Adam Smith* by Professor James Otteson (Yeshiva, US)
*Edmund Burke* by Professor Dennis O'Keeffe (Buckingham, UK)
*Alexis de Tocqueville* by Dr Alan S Kahan (Paris, France)
*Herbert Spencer* by Alberto Mingardi (Istituto Bruno Leoni, Italy)
*Ludwig von Mises* by Richard Ebeling (Trinity College)

*Joseph A. Schumpeter* by Professor John Medearis (Riverside, California, US)
*F. A. Hayek* by Dr Adam Tebble (UCL, UK)
*Michael Oakeshott* by Dr Edmund Neill (Oxford, UK)
*Karl Popper* by Dr Phil Parvin (Cambridge, UK)
*Ayn Rand* by Professor Mimi Gladstein (Texas, US)
*Milton Friedman* by Dr William Ruger (Texas State, US)
*James M. Buchanan* by Dr John Meadowcroft (King's College London, UK)
*The Modern Papacy* by Dr Samuel Gregg (Acton Institute, US)
*Robert Nozick* by Ralf Bader (St Andrews, UK)
*Russell Kirk* by Jon Pafford
*Murray Rothbard* by Gerard Casey

Of course, in any series of this nature, choices have to be made as to which thinkers to include and which to leave out. Two of the thinkers in the series – F. A. Hayek and James M. Buchanan – have written explicit statements rejecting the label 'conservative'. Similarly, other thinkers, such as David Hume and Karl Popper, may be more accurately described as classical liberals than either conservatives or libertarians. But these thinkers have been included because a full appreciation of this particular tradition of thought would be impossible without their inclusion; conservative and libertarian thought cannot be fully understood without some knowledge of the intellectual contributions of Hume, Hayek, Popper and Buchanan, among others. While no list of conservative and libertarian thinkers can be perfect, then, it is hoped that the volumes in this series come as close as possible to providing a comprehensive account of the key contributors to this particular tradition.

John Meadowcroft
King's College London

# The Salamanca School

André A. Alves
and
José M. Moreira

Major Conservative and
Libertarian Thinkers

Series Editor: John Meadowcroft

Volume 9

BLOOMSBURY
NEW YORK • LONDON • NEW DELHI • SYDNEY

**Bloomsbury Academic**
An imprint of Bloomsbury Publishing Plc

| 175 Fifth Avenue | 50 Bedford Square |
| New York | London |
| NY 10010 | WC1B 3DP |
| USA | UK |

www.bloomsbury.com

Hardback edition first published in 2010 by the Continuum International Publishing Group Inc.
This paperback edition published by Bloomsbury Academic 2013

© André A. Alves & José M. Moriera, 2013

All rights reserved. No part of this publication may be reproduced or transmitted in any form or by any means, electronic or mechanical, including photocopying, recording, or any information storage or retrieval system, without prior permission in writing from the publishers.

No responsibility for loss caused to any individual or organization acting on or refraining from action as a result of the material in this publication can be accepted by Bloomsbury Academic or the author.

**Library of Congress Cataloging-in-Publication Data**
A catalog record for this book is available from the Library of Congress.

ISBN: HB: 978-0-8264-2982-7
PB: 978-1-4411-7779-9

Typeset by Deanta Global Publishing Services, Chennai, India

To Alejandro Chafuen

# Contents

Series Editor's Preface ... xi
Acknowledgements ... xiii

## 1 Historical Context and Intellectual Biography ... 1
What Is the 'School of Salamanca'? ... 1
The Political and Intellectual Context
    of the School of Salamanca ... 6
The Decline of Scholasticism ... 11
Some Key Authors of the School of Salamanca ... 13
    *Francisco de Vitoria* ... 13
    *Domingo de Soto* ... 14
    *Martín de Azpilcueta* ... 15
    *Diego de Covarrubias y Leyva* ... 16
    *Tomás de Mercado* ... 17
    *Bartolomé de Las Casas* ... 18
    *Luis de Molina* ... 19
    *Juan de Mariana* ... 20
    *Francisco Suárez* ... 22

## 2 Critical Exposition ... 24
Philosophical and Political Foundations of the School ... 24
    *Thomism and natural law* ... 25
    *The European revival of Thomism and*
        *the Salamanca School* ... 30
    *Theological-political disputes* ... 34
Applied Political Thought ... 39
    *Individual rights and the common good* ... 39
    *The state and the limits of political power* ... 45

| | | |
|---|---|---|
| | *Legitimate resistance and tyrannicide* | 51 |
| | *Church and state* | 55 |
| | *International law and developments in Just War theory* | 59 |
| | The Ethical and Juridical Framework of the Market | 65 |
| | *Private property and trade* | 65 |
| | *Just price and the subjective theory of value* | 71 |
| | *Usury and interest* | 73 |
| | *Theories of banking* | 76 |
| | *Monetary theory and inflation* | 79 |
| | *Taxation and public finance* | 83 |
| **3** | **Reception and Influence of the Work** | 86 |
| | The Salamanca School and the New World | 86 |
| | *A revolutionary sermon in Hispaniola* | 87 |
| | *The social experiments of Bartolomé de Las Casas* | 90 |
| | *Just titles and the disputation between Las Casas and Sepúlveda* | 95 |
| | Assessing the Legacy of Las Casas and the Controversies over the New World | 100 |
| | Theological-Political Impact and Influence on Subsequent Authors | 102 |
| **4** | **Relevance of the Work Today** | 110 |
| | Political Philosophy, Law and History | 110 |
| | Political Economy and the Ethical Foundations of the Market | 113 |
| | Contemporary Catholic Social Thought | 115 |
| | International Relations and War | 117 |
| | Concluding Remarks | 119 |
| *Notes* | | 121 |
| *Bibliography* | | 139 |
| *Index* | | 149 |

# Series Editor's Preface

The Salamanca School describes the thought of the Catholic scholars directly and indirectly linked to the University of Salamanca in Spain in the sixteenth and seventeenth centuries, who developed the established philosophy of St Thomas Aquinas against the background of the rise of humanism and modern science, the Protestant reformation and the European colonization of the Americas. The Salamanca scholars, and particularly key figures like Francisco de Vitoria, Domingo de Soto, Martín de Azpilcueta, Tomás de Mercado, Bartolomé de Las Casas, Diego de Covarrubias y Leyva, Luis de Molina, Juan de Mariana and Francisco Suárez made a series of significant philosophical contributions, particularly to our understanding of ethics and economics. In this outstanding volume, André Azevedo Alves and José Manuel Moreira set out the thought of the Salamanca scholars, place that thought in its historical context, consider its reception by the contemporaries of the Salamanca thinkers and then discuss its continuing relevance.

Alves and Moreira show that the philosophical foundation of the Salamanca School was the idea of natural law: laws that are common to all mankind and always binding, such as the injunction against murder. The belief that natural law transcended human law meant that rulers (including kings and popes) who imposed unjust laws could be legitimately opposed and overthrown. The Salamanca scholars also defended private property in terms that anticipated Locke's later defence, set out the basic principles of international law and the grounds upon which war might be justified. Some astonishing contributions were also made in the field of economics, where the Salamanca authors were among the first to systematically develop the quantity theory of money that only gained wide acceptance in the second half of the twentieth century: the notion that the prices set within the economy have a positive relationship to the amount of money in circulation, so that inflation and deflation are the direct result of changes in the supply of money rather than other factors, such as the employment level or the rate of economic growth.

The sixteenth and seventeenth centuries witnessed an astonishing intellectual flourishing at the Iberian Peninsula centred at the University of Salamanca, comparable, perhaps, to the Scottish Enlightenment of the seventeenth and eighteenth centuries. Alves and Moreira show much we can still learn from the ideas that developed in this extraordinary intellectual milieu. Hence, although the School of Salamanca may not immediately spring to mind as a critical part of the conservative and libertarian traditions, this book demonstrates the important of these thinkers to conservatism, libertarianism and to political, social and economic thought more generally.

John Meadowcroft
King's College London

# Acknowledgements

The authors would like to thank first of all John Meadowcroft for his keen interest on the topic of this book and for the numerous and timely suggestions for improvement he provided. Notwithstanding all the assistance received, responsibility for all remaining shortcomings lies, of course, exclusively with the authors.

As often happens in book projects, close family members ended up bearing a significant share of the personal costs involved in the writing process. For their continued patience and support, André Azevedo Alves is thankful to Rosa Maria and to his parents Eusébio and Maria Celeste, while José Manuel Moreira wishes to thank Angélica and his daughter Teresa.

While a diverse range of ideas and interpretations were taken into account, the spirit of this book was particularly influenced by the earlier contributions of authors such as Raymond de Roover, Marjorie Grice-Hutchinson, Murray N. Rothbard and Jesús Huerta de Soto. Mention must also be made to Alejandro Chafuen, whose outstanding efforts to promote a more truthful understanding of liberty and the thought of the late scholastics amply justify that this book be dedicated to him.

André Azevedo Alves
London School of Economics and Political Science

José Manuel Moreira
Universidade de Aveiro

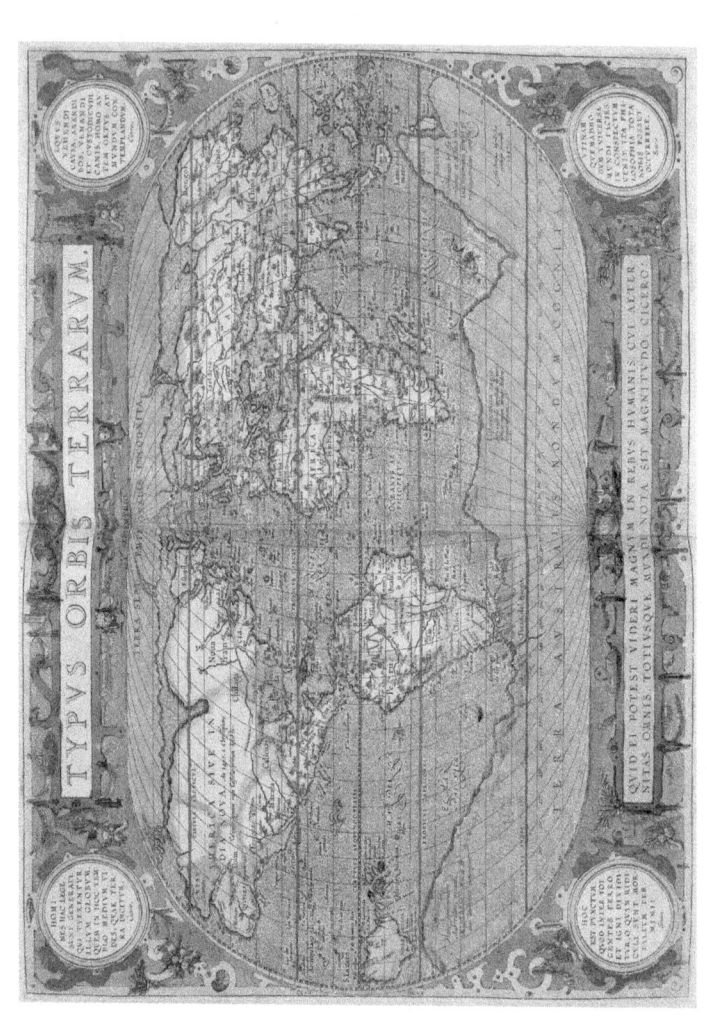

Chapter 1

# Historical Context and Intellectual Biography

## What Is the 'School of Salamanca'?

Just outside the United Nations building in New York stands a statue of a sixteenth-century Dominican theologian – Francisco de Vitoria. Those familiar with international law will know that Vitoria is justly credited as one of the founders of international law. But few will be aware that the same figure can also be credited with the foundation of a distinct School of theological, philosophical, political and economic thought to whose authors Hayek, in his Nobel lecture, referred to as 'those remarkable anticipators of modern economics, the Spanish schoolmen of the sixteenth century'.[1] That School is the subject of this book.

The expression 'School of Salamanca' is commonly used to refer to the group of Iberian scholastics of the sixteenth and early seventeenth century that were, more or less loosely, associated with the University of Salamanca. Although the Dominican – and distinguished Thomist – Francisco de Vitoria (c. 1483–1546) is usually credited as the founder of the School, it was not limited to Dominican theologians, with members of other religious orders – particularly Jesuits – also providing significant contributions to the development of Salamancan ideas and intellectual influence.

As is often the case with the intellectual grouping into schools or paradigms, the concept and delimitation of a distinct Salamanca School is not without controversy. To mention two of the most notable dissentions, Pribram (1983, 28–29) argues for setting the (Jesuits) Luis de Molina and Juan de Lugo apart from the rest of the (mostly Dominican) School of Salamanca while Chafuen (2003) prefers the denomination 'Hispanic Scholastics' because some of the most important Iberian authors of this period conducted their studies at universities other than Salamanca.[2] It is undeniable that, for example, authors as relevant as Luis de Molina and Francisco Suárez were Jesuits and had the largest shares of their productive years in Portugal (at the universities of Évora and Coimbra) but nevertheless they can be associated with the Salamancan tradition to the extent they undertook studies there and have carried forth that tradition in their works, not only in terms of the themes they studied but also in the scholastic approach they adopted. It is also true that on some issues there are substantial differences of opinion between authors associated with the Salamancan approach, but the same can certainly be said of most schools of thought. Despite its possible shortcomings, the use of the name School of Salamanca to identify this group of philosophers of natural law and moral theologians enjoys a considerably long and solid tradition in the literature, dating back at least to the work of Wilhelm Endemann in 1874.[3]

In this context, it seems reasonable to continue to refer to the Salamanca School. Chafuen (2003) is probably right when stating that 'Hispanic Scholastics' is, in some sense, a more precise definition but it also carries two significant disadvantages when compared with continuing to refer to the School of Salamanca: first, it is less informative to the extent it omits reference to the most important academic intellectual centre of the time and second, it unnecessarily discards the rich and respectable historical use of the expression in many instances of the literature on political philosophy and economic theory. The expression Salamanca School is used throughout this book in a relatively broad sense, including members of different religious orders and with different degrees of connection and proximity with the University of Salamanca and with the work of Francisco de Vitoria. The Salamancan authors considered here share essential similarities in terms of the regeneration of the scholastic method, their main authoritative sources (Greek philosophers – particularly Aristotle – the Roman jurists, the Old and New Testaments, Christian Patristic literature and earlier scholastics – above all St Thomas Aquinas) and many features of their outlook on political and economic issues. These characteristics – more than the amount of time they spent at Salamanca or the extent to which they can be considered direct followers of Francisco de Vitoria – are the main identifying elements of the authors included in the Salamanca School.

Used in this sense, the Salamanca School can be said to range roughly from the first decades of the sixteenth century to the first half of the seventeenth century, when its activity in the Iberian Peninsula (although not necessarily its direct and indirect influence elsewhere) gradually started to decline. A period during which its main authors taught not only in Salamanca but also in Alcalá de Henares and other Spanish universities as well as in Portuguese universities like Coimbra and Évora.

One of the main concerns of the Salamancan scholastics was to take into account the interconnection of all areas of human knowledge and contribute to a unified understanding of the world and its laws. All of them had, first of all, pastoral concerns and often intended to address ethical problems that arose both for politicians and businessmen in light of the teachings of moral theology. But their work was generally carried out with the concern of incorporating a correct understanding of the laws of political economy and their inevitable implications and not – as unfortunately happens too often when dealing with ethical and political philosophy issues – through well sounding pronouncements that neglect those very same laws.[4]

But the contribution of the Salamancans was not limited to economic theory and theological issues, although they did exert a powerful influence in matters like the replacement of Peter Lombard's *Sentences* by Aquinas' *Summa Theologica* as the main object of study, a change that was a key feature in the revival of Thomism.[5] The interests of the members of Salamanca School spread to areas related to the main social and political issues of their time, including what we would now call individual rights, international law, just war and peace, the moral legitimacy of New World explorations and conquests, business and financial ethics and the responsibility of governments and civil society towards poverty and mendacity. The writings of the scholastics associated with the School of Salamanca dealt with all these issues in an integrated framework of natural law and moral theology. This means that their contributions to political, economic and social thought must be considered in that context to be properly understood but one of their main distinguishing features is that they truly brought philosophy and theology to applied social and policy issues in a systematic fashion.

It is important at this point to consider in what light and to what extent can the Salamanca scholastics be considered 'conservative' or 'libertarian'. They certainly would not have self-identified as such at the time, given that these categories (as we now conceive of them) were the product of later intellectual and political developments. Nevertheless they did contribute and develop very important ideas and insights that later came to assume a central role in those intellectual traditions. More importantly: they often did so from a coherent perspective that always sought to integrate theological, philosophical, political and economic knowledge. Revisiting their teachings is valuable not only in terms of better understanding the genealogy of ideas but also as a source of alternative integrated perspectives on contemporary issues. Regardless of normative political preferences, a significant part of the arguments put forth by the authors within the Salamanca School are certain to interest – and in some cases surprise – contemporary readers.

Simultaneously, familiarizing oneself with the main political and economic contributions of the School of Salamanca is also fundamental to understand the policy implications of one of the main pillars of the Western political thought tradition, namely that line of inquiry that built upon the methods and insights of St Thomas Aquinas. The Salamancan theologians and natural law philosophers were firmly in the inherited Thomist tradition that in large part defined 'Western' political thought. They combine a strong adherence to the scholastic methods of rigorous deductive and speculative reasoning and to traditional authoritative sources with the objective to present, develop and apply Christian doctrine to the most salient issues of their time. In this process, they find themselves in the singular position of promoting a revival of Thomism while at the same time anticipating some of the decisive elements of the transition to the modern period. Through the analysis of the thought of the Salamancans it is also possible to gain valuable insights on how that process occurred. This involves understanding what elements were carried forth and which were either abandoned or forgotten. In many ways – but particularly though its influence on modern philosophy – the specific shape of this transition to modernity also determined important features of contemporary political thought.

Given the extremely vast array of possibilities and scope to be covered in a work that seeks to provide a general succinct overview of the main contributions of the Salamanca School and the objectives of this collection, the approach taken here is to highlight and present the ideas most interesting for the contemporary conservative and libertarian traditions. At the same time, adequate attention will be paid to tensions and conflicts in those ideas, as well as to ways in which they fundamentally or partially differ from contemporary interpretations.

The structure of the book is as follows: the remaining part of this chapter presents a brief overview of the political and intellectual context of the School of Salamanca as a whole, followed by a series of short biographical notes on some of its most notable figures; the second chapter includes an exposition of the main philosophical and political foundations of the Salamanca School and a presentation of its most salient contributions in terms of applied political thought and the ethical and juridical framework of what we would now call the extended market order; the third chapter deals with the reception of the work of the Salamancans at the time and their influence in subsequent periods; the fourth chapter discusses the contemporary relevance of the contributions of the Salamanca School; the chapters are followed by a bibliography that aims to serve as a first step for those interested in deepening their knowledge of the topics covered throughout the book.

## The Political and Intellectual Context of the School of Salamanca

The golden age of Iberia – that largely coincided with the time of the authors considered in this volume – took place after a movement of global journeys of navigation and exploration in which Portugal and Spain were pioneers.

In the case of Portugal – an independent nation-state since the twelfth century – the major points in this movement were the exploration of the African coastline, the discovery of the maritime route to India and the (European) discovery of Brazil. In Spain, the 1469 marriage of the 'Catholic Kings' Fernando (of Aragón) and Isabel (of Castilla) gave way to a process of re-conquest and unification that eventually led to the expulsion of the Arabs from the Iberian peninsula in 1492, the very same year of Columbus' pioneering journey to America. Columbus' voyage is perhaps the most notable result of a policy of maritime expeditions that led to the European settlement in America, although the initially stated aim of the expeditions was that of finding a maritime route to India by navigating westward. The increasingly aggressive competition between the Iberian peoples for the discovery and exploration of the 'New World' in this period was also the root cause of the establishment of a treaty that settled the latent conflict between the two states. The result was the division of the World between Portugal and Spain with the signature of the famous *Treaty of Tordesillas* in 1494. After the arrival of Columbus to America, the treaty determined the division of New World territories into two distinct spheres of influence, with the Western part belonging to Spain and the Eastern part to Portugal. It is this division established in the treaty that lies at the root of the separation that nowadays is still largely present in Latin America and roughly corresponds to the frontier lines between Portuguese-speaking Brazil and the Spanish-speaking countries of Latin America.

The reign of Fernando and Isabel also gave rise to the enlargement of the powers of Castilla, which was accompanied by the hiring of thousands of people to the several administrative, military and judicial ranks of the expanding state. The new lawyers, administrators, tax collectors, military specialists – amongst other professionals – were all seen as requiring appropriate education and formation for the increasingly challenging tasks they had to deal with in their (often newly created) positions. As would be expected, this process created conditions to solidify the grip of Castilla on the Spanish territories but it also coexisted with an intellectual climate of openness to new knowledge and new realities that generated favourable conditions for the so-called Spanish *'Siglo de Oro'* ('Golden Century', the period approximately between 1525 and 1640). This period included the 60 years (1580–1640) during which Portugal was unified in a single kingdom with Spain, as a consequence of the death of D. Sebastião and of the marriage – celebrated in Salamanca – of the Prince of Astúrias, D. Felipe (later Felipe II of Spain and Felipe I of Portugal), with D. Maria, daughter of D. João III of Portugal and of his wife Catarina, sister of the Emperor Carlos V.[6]

Isabel and Fernando are often credited for having ruled not so much with the aid of the 'noble' as with the counsel of the 'learned'. In fact, the growth of the importance of the universities in Spain (as well as in Portugal) can be explained in large part both by the interest of the noble – that hoped to continue to hold on to political power and social influence and status – and by the demand for formal education by second-born (and in some cases illegitimate) children of wealthy families. Higher education was increasingly regarded as a means of personal promotion and a tool to gain access to attractive administrative positions, both in civil and religious institutions. Hence the flourishing of the universities that supplied adequate degrees for those purposes, even though higher education required either substantial economic resources or the support of a religious Order.[7]

This trend paved the way for greater freedom and participation in the universities and even to institutional competition for the supply of the best teaching and the most adequate competences between the religious Orders associated with academia, particularly the Dominicans and the recently established Jesuits. Even though some regard the universities as subordinated to the needs of the State,[8] the truth is that the elitist processes of hiring can also be regarded as contributing to the creation of a competitive environment that fostered academic improvement and that may be part of the explanation for the tremendous scholarly productivity during this period.

Whatever the relative importance of the different causal factors, Castille experienced a period of great educational activity and innovation and the University of Salamanca was at the core of that process. As noted by Montes (1998, pp. 25–26), the fundamentally pedagogical vocation of the University of Salamanca (well expressed in its motto '*Omnium scientiarum princeps Salmantica docet*', which meant to emphasize that Salamanca led in the teaching of all the sciences) was at the time reflected in a set of valuable characteristics: a carefully designed lecturing model, the focus on personal study and library work, the educational duties assigned to a small minority of selected students, the emphasis on preparing students for decision-making and leadership roles, the humanistic programmes and the moral and religious education (in line with the statutes that established that the University should also be a place for the students to learn virtue, good customs and composure).

The relative peace in the Iberian Peninsula during the *Siglo de Oro*, coupled with favourable demographic, political and economic factors all contributed to the educational developments in Castilla – and particularly in Salamanca – during the period but there are at least five other relevant conditions that should be taken into consideration.[9] First, the development of the printed press made possible a drastic reduction in the costs of producing books and allowed a much wider diffusion of scholarly materials. This was particularly important for institutions that were already undergoing an expansionary movement due to other factors. Second, the Iberian Peninsula at this time benefited from the cultural legacy and interplay of Christian, Jewish and Muslim civilizations. Third, both Salamanca and Alcalá were privileged centres of reception of humanist ideas. While this humanism in many ways clashed with traditional scholasticism it nevertheless developed in those centres in a way that – at least initially – was not incompatible with the maintenance of classical and biblical studies.[10] This ascension of humanism and the movement of scholastic renewal cannot of course be separated from the religious confrontation between Protestants and Catholics taking place throughout Europe at the time, a factor that also played an important role in the affirmation of the School of Salamanca. Under the challenge of Protestant reformers who proclaimed to be returning to the original meaning of biblical texts, there was a widely felt need on the part of Catholics to renew and reinvigorate the Church's teachings and improve the education of both the clergy and the laity. While the Counter-Reformation was undoubtedly 'far more complex than simply a response to the Protestant challenge' and was largely a culmination of a series of trends and unresolved disputes dating back to the late medieval period, it is also clear that the climate of religious confrontation fuelled the mobilization of universities and intellectual resources.[11] This was particularly true after the three sessions of the Council of Trent (1545–1547, 1549–1551, 1561–1563) came to a firm and clear rejection of the Protestant Reformation on all major disputed issues.[12] The creation and rapid growth of the Society of Jesus (officially recognized by Pope Paul III's 1540 *Regimini Militantis Ecclesiae* bull)[13] also came to play an important role in the theological and political-philosophical disputes of the period, despite the fact that the original 'charters' of the organization did not anticipate the prominence Jesuits scholars would come to assume in those domains.[14] It is worth noting that although initially composed mostly of Dominicans, the School of Salamanca came to include a significant number of Jesuits in leading roles, particularly from the late sixteenth century onwards. Finally, the Iberian maritime campaigns of overseas discovery and exploration constitute a fifth factor of educational and intellectual stimulus that must be considered in its own right. The discoveries led to a cosmographical revolution that preceded the Copernican scientific revolution and while it had implications for many other universities, it is certainly possible to argue that the University of Salamanca was at the time a privileged forum for the discussion and interplay of scientific ideas with the experience, practical knowledge and new challenges posed by the explorations of Spanish and Portuguese navigators.[15] The Iberian Peninsula was in this period a central location for the exchange not only of goods but also of ideas in the context of an increasingly open world and it was in response to the associated new challenges – both internal and external – that the political and economic thought of Salamancan scholastics achieved its maximum expression. Marjorie Grice-Hutchinson (1978, p. 73) offers a useful summary of this line of reasoning:

> The sixteenth and early seventeenth centuries were in every sense a golden age for Spain. How far, if at all, that great flowering of art and literature was stimulated by the inflow of American treasure can only be a matter for conjecture. It is otherwise in the case of learning, where the most notable Spanish achievements were closely related to the conquest of the Indies and all that followed from it.
>
> Since the completion of the Reconquest, the Spanish universities had come to occupy a foremost place among those of Europe. In particular, the University of Salamanca was famed for the brilliant teachers who were attracted to its chairs: grammarians, poets, historians and, above all, theologians, philosophers and jurists.

The prominence of the School of Salamanca can in some ways be seen as the intellectual correspondence to a period in which the Iberian Peninsula – with roughly a perimeter of 4,500 kilometres of which 90 per cent run alongside sea coast and only 450 kilometres link it to the main European continent – became in many aspects the centre of the world. The universal dimension and new centrality provided by the discovery of the New World are essential to understand the position of the University of Salamanca at the time and its role as focal point for numerous thinkers and ideas in the main domains of human knowledge at the time.

## The Decline of Scholasticism

Unsurprisingly, the decline of the Salamanca School largely coincided with what Pagden (2002, pp. 82–87) describes as 'the decline of the Iberian world'. Ultimately the far-reaching Iberian global empire proved unsustainable and slowly fell apart, either through capture by the English, French and Dutch rivals or – at a later stage – due to former colonies becoming new independent countries. As pointed out by Pagden (2002, p. 84):

> Burdened with the need to hold together diverse, overextended states, Philip II and his successors Philip III and IV had been overly concerned with the short-term gains of war and insufficiently mindful of the long-term economic needs of the various peoples of which their monarchy was composed.

In addition to military and administrative problems, the huge quantities of gold and silver brought from America induced serious inflation problems in the Iberian Peninsula, while the focus on conquest and precious metals distorted economy activity in other sectors.[16] By the nineteenth century, Portugal and Spain still held considerable overseas territories but the extent of their global reach and power was incomparably lower to what it had been in the sixteenth and early seventeenth centuries.

In conjunction with the geopolitical and economic factors, the decline of scholasticism also reflected broader intellectual trends, both inside and outside the Catholic Church. In spite of the considerable successes achieved by the Catholic Counter-Reformation, in the long run Protestants and secularists ended up prevailing and this had very negative implications for scholasticism. As noted by Rothbard (2006, pp. 128–131), the wide reach of scholasticism had been closely linked with the (relative) unity of the Universal Church and with the wide use of Latin. Both elements had fostered a truly international community of scholars and academic institutions and as both of them were gradually weakened in the wake of the Protestant Reformation, scholasticism also suffered considerably.

Furthermore, the intellectual and political moods of the Renaissance proved largely inimical to scholasticism and its methods, as it was 'a philosophical tradition which had by then come to be closely associated with the old order'.[17] In political philosophy, despite the contributions and direct and indirect influences of the late Iberian scholastics,[18] modernity would ultimately largely put aside traditional Aristotelic and Thomist approaches and rely instead on rather more secular and pragmatist explorations of the concept of 'reason of state'.[19]

A combination of several factors therefore played a role in the decline of scholasticism and particularly of traditional Thomist approaches both in Catholic and non-Catholic countries. As summed up by Haldane (2004, p. 7):

> In 1772, Jesuits were suppressed o the order of the Pope, and in the next decade Catholicism itself was battered by the French Revolution and by the rise of secularism. The new political thinking was anti-theocratic, anti-clerical, broadly democratic, and at best deistic, though often atheist. It is hardly surprising, therefore, that a system of thought born of medieval Catholicism did not flourish in these circumstances.

## Some Key Authors of the School of Salamanca

The following series of short biographical notes on some of the most notable figures of the School of Salamanca seeks to complement the general presentation of the School and to better contextualize the contribution of its authors. The main criterion for inclusion is the extent to which the contributions of each scholastic are explored in subsequent chapters. It should nevertheless be recognized that such a choice of authors always involves a degree of subjectivity and is in this case also subordinated to the aim of outlining the most relevant contributions from the perspective of contemporary libertarian and conservative thought. The selection should therefore not be interpreted as a general judgement on the relative importance of the contributions of each thinker when compared with those not included in this short list.

**Francisco de Vitoria**

Although the exact timing of his birth is unknown it is estimated that Francisco de Vitoria was probably born in 1483 and died in 1546. He completed his first academic studies in Burgos, where he also entered the Dominican Order in 1504. Vitoria was then sent by his superiors to the Collège de St Jacques at the University of Paris where he pursued his studies and also became a lecturer. In Paris he was greatly influenced by Pierre Crockaert and developed a profound admiration for St Thomas Aquinas, to the extent that he came to personally prepare an edition of the *Secunda secundae* of Aquinas' *Summa Theologiae*. In 1523 he returned to Spain, holding a position in Valladolid until 1526 when he was elected to the prestigious prime chair of theology at the University of Salamanca, which he held for two decades.[20]

In Salamanca, Vitoria enacted several important curricular reforms promoting a revival of Thomism and of the scholastic method. By moving away from Ockhamism and nominalism – which had been extremely influent throughout the Middle Ages – Vitoria gave a decisive contribution to the philosophical and theological renewal that swept Iberian universities after the Council of Trent. By the time of Vitoria's death, nearly thirty of his former students held professorships in Spanish universities and his influence rapidly extended to Latin America, and particularly to Mexico in large part due to his disciple Alonso de la Vera Cruz, one of the first great American philosophers.[21]

Given his scholarly achievements, his broad (direct and indirect) academic influence and the attention he paid to current issues of the time such as the origin of political authority, the legitimacy of Spanish campaigns in America and the status of Amerindians and their communities, Vitoria is usually considered the founder of the School of Salamanca. His philosophical, ethical and political contributions are deeply linked with sociological, anthropological and juridical insights and particularly his reflections on the legitimacy of the conduct of states and individuals in the course of international affairs give him a strong claim to being one of the founding fathers of international law. The main features of his political contributions are well patent in three of his surviving *relectiones*: *De potestate civili* (on civil power), *De indis* (on the Indians) and *De iure belli* (on the law of war).[22] Also of special interest are his commentaries to Aquinas' *Summa*, particularly on law and justice.[23]

**Domingo de Soto**

Domingo de Soto was born in 1495 in Segovia and was perhaps the most influential theologian of the School of Salamanca. Soto studied at Alcalá before moving to Paris where, after an initial formation framed by nominalism, he would eventually be converted to Francisco de Vitoria's line of Thomism. On his return to Spain, Soto lectured at Alcalá but left the University in 1524 in order to enter the Dominican Order. He would eventually be elected to a chair of theology in Salamanca in 1532, a position

Domingo de Soto occupied until 1545, when he was selected by Charles V to be the imperial theologian at the Council of Trent. After the first interruption of the Council, Soto became confessor and spiritual director to the emperor but gave up his highly influential position in 1550 in order to return to Salamanca and pursue his academic career. In 1552 Soto became the holder of the prime chair of theology at the University of Salamanca. He died in Salamanca in 1560.[24]

Domingo de Soto's most significant work in terms of political, juridical and economic thought is *De iustitia et iure*, which was first published in 1553–1554 and was the subject of 27 further editions in the following five decades. Soto's work covers not only traditional issues of justice but also many applied problems related with business activities and with the Spanish actions in the New World. In several of his works, Soto also devoted substantial attention to poverty laws, their consequences and the most advisable ways for the public authorities and the community to deal with beggars. He opposed the prohibition of begging but generally trusted more in the potential of free individual and communitarian action than in the responses of public authorities and favoured the reliance on traditional institutions associated with the Church to address those problems.[25]

### Martín de Azpilcueta

Martín de Azpilcueta was born in 1492 in Navarra (close to the Spanish border with France) and was often referred to as *Doctor Navarrus*. He held a chair at the University of Salamanca and in 1538 was sent by Charles V to teach at the University of Coimbra, where he lectured on international law along the lines of his contemporary and friend Francisco de Vitoria.[26]

Azpilcueta's *Manual de confessores y penitentes* (dedicated to his patroness Princess Joana, sister of Philip II) was first published in Coimbra in 1553 and achieved great success as a manual of moral theology. It was successively republished in Portuguese, Spanish, Latin and Italian in the late sixteenth and early seventeenth centuries. It is noteworthy that a 1556 edition of the *Manual* published in Salamanca included an appendix of additional commentaries on foreign exchange and usury that includes what is often considered the first clear exposition of the quantity theory of money.[27]

Recognized as an eminent authority on canon law, Doctor Navarrus moved to Rome where he acted as an advisor to Popes Pius V, Gregory XIII and Sixtus V. Martín de Azpilcueta lived over 90 years and passed away in 1586.

### Diego de Covarrubias y Leyva

The jurist, theologian and historian Diego de Covarrubias y Leyva was born in Toledo in 1512, and he is sometimes credited with being one of the founders of international law, jointly with Francisco de Vitoria of whom he was one the most brilliant disciples in Salamanca.[28] His father was Alonso de Covarrubias y Leyva, one of the most famous architects of his time, and Diego started his studies in Salamanca at the age of 10. He studied law under Martín de Azpilcueta and theology under Francisco de Vitoria and Domingo de Soto. In 1539 he successfully defended his doctoral dissertation in which he argued that it is in knowledge and in culture – and not in war – that lies the true source of greatness of the nations. In 1540 he was appointed to the position of Professor of Canon Law and in 1548 he was appointed by Charles V to a prominent position in the Chancellery of Granada. From 1560 until his death in 1577, Covarrubias also had an influential role in Spanish politics at the highest level. In 1572 he was appointed President of the Council of Castile and later to the presidency of the Council of State. At some points in time during this period he was probably the most influential political figure in Spain. Covarrubias was also bishop of Ciudad Rodrigo, in which capacity he took part in the Council of Trent, where he played a key role in drafting some of the main reforms approved. After his return to Spain, in 1565 he moved to become bishop of Segovia.

During his academic career, he published numerous works on a wide range of theological, juridical and historical subjects (during his own lifetime more than 30 editions of his books were published). Covarrubias influential works' include *Variarum Resolutionum* and *Quaestiones practicae*, and much of his written contributions reflect the combination of his academic education and research at Salamanca with the practical experience derived from the administrative positions he held during his life. In addition to his important contributions to law, theology and history, Covarrubias also provided important contributions for the theory of value and the theory of prices.

**Tomás de Mercado**

Relatively little is known with certainty about Tomás de Mercado's life but it is estimated that he was born sometime c. 1530. He moved to Mexico in his youth, where he studied and joined the Dominican Order in 1552. In 1562/63 he headed to Spain to complete his studies at the University of Salamanca and later lectured on philosophy, moral theology and law at Salamanca and Sevilla. He died in 1575 on his return to Mexico.[29]

Mercado's most famous book is his *Suma de tratos y contratos*, printed for the first time in Salamanca in 1569, with an enlarged re-edition in Seville in 1571 and 1578 and translated to Italian in 1591. This *Suma* is aimed primarily at traders and clergy and constitutes essentially a manual of commercial and financial practices that seeks to frame business activities in the context of the pursuit of the common good.[30] At the same time, Mercado offers a valuable historical description of commercial and financial activity in his time and contributes important insights in the domain of economic theory, anticipating to some extent the formulation of the quantity theory of money.[31] Although Mercado was a theologian, his economic writings assumed a practical – more than speculative – nature, perhaps as a consequence of his active contact with the commercial sphere (as was customary at the time, in addition to his academic activities he also acted as an advisor on economic, juridical and ethical issues). The large scope of practical knowledge of business practices held by the author certainly contributed to the establishment of the *Suma de tratos y contratos* as something of a moral and practical guidebook for traders in the sixteenth century.[32] But the popularity achieved by Mercado's manual was probably also due to his able combination of scholastic sources with insightful empirical observation and realistic advice formulated in an expressive and occasionally even humoristic style.[33]

**Bartolomé de Las Casas**

Bartolomé de Las Casas was born in 1474 in Seville, although his family was of French origin. Las Casas pursued his studies at the University of Salamanca and became a lawyer. In 1502, he made his first trip to the New World and became an active participant in the Spanish *encomienda* system of colonization he would later come to condemn.[34] Having already been ordained priest, in 1513 Las Casas served as chaplain during the Spanish conquest of Cuba. The participation in the Cuban campaign, together with the influence of Father Montesinos, raised doubts in Las Casas' conscience and eventually led him to denounce the conquest and enslavement of the American Indians. He gave up the lands and the Indian serfs that were until then entrusted to him and started to preach against the *encomienda* system. As part of his active campaigning Las Casas proposed alternative schemes of colonization and was allowed by the Spanish Crown to make a trial in territories corresponding to present-day Venezuela. The plan – which included the importation of African slaves – was an abysmal failure but Las Casas' determination was not broken.[35]

In 1522 Las Casas joined a Dominican convent at Santo Domingo and began writing his *Historia de las Indias*, where he painted an extremely gruesome and cruel picture of Spanish colonization in America. After a period studying theology and law, Las Casas returned to active campaigning in the 1530s. In 1537 he led the peaceful conversion to Christianity of warring

Indian tribes in Guatemala and in 1540 returned to Spain to continue his campaign for the abolition of the *encomienda* system. His campaigning was influential for the 1542 promulgation of the New Laws of the Indies, limiting to a significant degree the serfdom of the American Indians. The new laws caused significant agitation and indignation in the American colonies and the intense protest of Spanish settlers eventually led to their partial revocation.

In 1544 Las Casas became bishop of Chiapas but would return to Spain only a few years later. There he continued his active campaign for the rights of Indians and the controversy culminated with the famous 1550 debate that posed Las Casas against Ginés de Sepúlveda (and had Domingo de Soto as one of the judges, although the final outcome is not clear).

Las Casas died in Madrid in 1566 and although he led an extremely active life his scholarly contributions are relatively minor when compared with those of the Salamancan Doctors. Still, even though Las Casas can perhaps be classified as more of an activist and campaigner than a scholar, his actions constitute a fine example of the practical implications, impact and results of the philosophical and political contributions of the School of Salamanca.

**Luis de Molina**

Luis de Molina was born in Cuenca c. 1535 and conducted his first studies in Salamanca and Alcalá. He joined the Society of Jesus at the age of 18 and spent most of his active academic years in Portugal, first at the University of Coimbra, where he studied and taught, and then at the University of Évora. Molina returned to Spain in the early 1590s and died in 1600.[36] At the University of Évora (established in 1559 by Cardinal D. Henrique), Molina was elected to the prime chair of theology in the early 1570s and had a long and notable tenure.

Molina's works – which came to be studied and discussed in the major European universities and spanned lively discussions and aggressive rivalry between supporters and opposers of

*Molinism* – include several extended commentaries on Aquinas' *Summa theologiae* (mostly derived from his lectures), but it is generally recognized that his most influential and controversial contribution is the *Concordia*. With a first edition published in Lisbon in 1588 (*Concordia liberi arbitrii cum gratiae donis, divina praescientia, providentia, praedestinatione et reprobatione*), it was the result of nearly three decades of work by Molina and made him one of the most famous and controversial European theologians and philosophers at the end of sixteenth century.[37] The *Concordia* deals with the difficult issue of reconciling free will and divine grace and can also be viewed as an attempt to offer a vindication on logical grounds of the doctrine of the Council of Trent that recognized the permanence of human free will under the action of efficacious grace. The *Concordia* generated heated controversy even before its publication with Molina eventually being denounced to the Inquisition. The controversy over *Molinism* raged on for years although his teachings were eventually exonerated by the Holy See.[38]

In addition to his theological and philosophical works (and controversies), Molina's contributions extended into the domains of politics, economics and law. His *De iustitia et iure* presents both his general theory of law as well as several distinct applications to problems of his time, covering issues such as the relationship between Church and State, the legitimacy of political power and numerous economic questions.

**Juan de Mariana**

Born in 1536 in Talavera de la Reina (Spain), Juan de Mariana was simultaneously theologian, historian, political philosopher, economist and holder of a profound knowledge of classic culture and classic languages: Latin, Greek and Hebrew. Mariana studied at the University of Alcalá and entered the Society of Jesus in 1554. In 1561 he was called by his superiors to teach in Rome, and after that lectured in Sicily and at the University of Paris, where he held a chair of theology. He returned to Toledo, in Spain, in 1574 where he devoted most of his time to writing until his death in 1624.

Mariana is the author of many books with original versions in Latin but often translated to Spanish by the author himself. In addition to his monumental *Histôria de España* (a major work on Spanish history), his two most significant works are *De rege et regis institutione* and the *De monetae mutatione*. The literary evolution of Mariana show a gradual evolution of his thought on political, economic and social issues to what would be contemporarily described as more libertarian positions, particularly in his latter writings.[39] As will be elaborated in the next chapter of this book, some of the strongest scholastic defences of economic freedom, sound money and the limitation of political power are indeed to be found in Mariana's works.

*De rege et regis institutione* – written at the expense of King Philip II for the education of the royal princes and dedicated to Philip III who had assumed the throne in the meantime – put forth Mariana's famous defence of the legitimacy of deposing and killing tyrant rulers. The book was tolerated in Spain but generated great scandal in France, as it was interpreted as justifying the assassination of the French monarch. In 1610, by order of the Parliament, the book was publicly burnt in Paris at the hands of the executioner although Mariana continued to benefit from the protection of the Spanish crown.[40]

Mariana's courage and convictions are equally present in his vehement denunciation of the debasement of currency in his *De monetae mutatione*. In this work, Mariana criticized the governmental practice of obtaining stealth fiscal revenues by reducing the precious metal content of the coins in circulation and inflating their number. The book was immediately persecuted by the Spanish authorities and eventually led to an investigation by the Inquisition. Mariana recognized he had been the author of the writings and took responsibility for them but refused to change their contents or retract his denouncement of the depreciation of currency by the State. He was however forced to commit to abstain from republishing them and – at age 73 – was confined to a Franciscan monastery. After one year of imprisonment, Mariana was freed and returned to Toledo, where he died in 1624.[41]

**Francisco Suárez**

Francisco Suárez, sometimes referred to as *Doctor Eximius*, was born in 1548 in Granada and died in Lisbon in 1617 after a distinguished and influential career as theologian and philosopher. Having entered the Society of Jesus in 1564, Suárez studied philosophy and theology at the University of Salamanca from 1564 to 1570. After teaching at several Spanish universities, Suárez moved to Rome in 1580 where he had Leonard Lessius (1554–1623) as disciple. In 1585 he returned to Spain, teaching first at Alcalá and then at the University of Salamanca. In the 1590s Suárez was sent by Philip II to the University of Coimbra where he spent the rest of his active teaching career.[42]

Suárez' prestige was such that the Holy See encouraged him to write a refutation of the errors of King James I of England when he defended the English oath of allegiance against Rome and particularly against the attacks mounted by Cardinal Bellarmine. This task was at the root of one of Suárez' most influential works in terms of political thought: his 1613 *Defensio fidei*, in which he sought to defend the Catholic position from the Anglican claims. In 1614 the book was promptly banned by the Parliament of Paris for promoting doctrines that opposed the power of sovereigns. Not surprisingly, the English king also ordered it to be burned in London.[43] Suárez also provided important contributions to political and juridical thought – and particularly to international law – in his 1612 *Tractatus de Legibus ac Deo Legislatore*.

Suárez' most influential philosophical contributions can be found in his *Disputationes Metaphysicae* (published in 1597), in which he presented an ordered synthesis of the main metaphysical topics and, to a large extent, furthered and solidified the approach developed by Luis de Molina in his *Concordia*.[44]

His overall philosophical approach became known as '*Suarism*', with special classes on his thought later being founded in universities such as Valladolid, Salamanca and Alcalá.[45]

Overall, Suárez' work can be regarded as providing a relatively homogeneous synthesis of the corpus of Thomist thought developed by the sixteenth-century Salamancans.[46] Through the widespread divulgation of his own writings and through the work of disciples like Lessius, Suárez' teachings' gradually spread throughout Europe and the rest of the world, while, at the same time, the status of the Iberian Peninsula as the pre-eminent global intellectual centre was on the decline.[47]

Chapter 2

# Critical Exposition

The critical exposition of the thought of the Salamanca School is divided here in three main areas. The first deals with the philosophical and political foundations of the School, with a particular emphasis on its Thomist roots and the influence of the challenges of the theological-political disputes of the period. The second presents an overview of thought of the late Iberian scholastics in the domains of applied political thought to which they provided more significant contributions. The third is focused on matters of political economy and analyses the contributions of the Salamanca School in what concerns the ethical and juridical framework of the market.

## Philosophical and Political Foundations of the School

The works of the Salamanca School in the domain of politics reflect a wide range of influences but it is possible to draw out two as the most important. The first is the natural law tradition dating back to Aristotle, carried forth by Roman authors, incorporated and adapted into Christian thought by earlier scholastics, and famously systematized by St Thomas Aquinas. The second is the troubled European context of the time with its intense theological and political disputes, particularly those that arose from the Protestant Reformation. Understanding the European revival of Thomism is particularly important for contextualizing the works of Vitoria and other Dominican members of the Salamanca

School (although not only for them) while the theological-political confrontations of the time were likely the main factor leading to the creation of the Society of Jesus, which provided most of the prominent later members of the Salamanca School. Both factors, addressed in this section, are important to understand the theoretical framework and the mindset with which the late Iberian scholastics approached contemporary polemics and proposed solutions to the pressing practical issues of the day.

**Thomism and natural law**

The crucial importance of the teachings of St Thomas Aquinas for the School of Salamanca can be immediately apprehended if one considers that most of the main works of the late Iberian scholastics appear under the form of extended commentaries on Aquinas' *Summa theologiae*. But the influence of Aquinas was not limited to serving as a base for further theoretical enquiry – the late Iberian scholastics also generally made an effort to address the most important contemporary problems of the time by making use of a Thomist framework of analysis. When the circumstances posed new problems that required innovative solutions, the teachings of Aquinas – and not other sources of the time – were generally the starting point of reflection. Complex (and sensitive) matters like the issue of the proper relationship between Church and State were addressed explicitly through the lenses of Thomistic political philosophy which replaced other popular (but less sound) medieval approaches to these problems.[1]

Such is the perceived influence of Aquinas that in his influential work on *The Foundations of Modern Political Thought*, Quentin Skinner (1978) goes as far as including his treatment of the authors of the School of Salamanca under the label 'The revival of Thomism' – an option that can be reasonably defended. In order to understand the philosophical and political foundations of the Salamanca School it is therefore important to have at least some basic notions about Aquinas and his thought. By bearing those notions in mind it will be possible to understand the way some of Aquinas' ideas came to be adopted (and adapted) by these later scholastics and how they played a crucial role in shaping their intellectual areas of enquiry and their own philosophical and political thought.

Thomas Aquinas (1225–1274) was born into an aristocratic family in Southern Italy and received his early education at the Benedictine monastery of Monte Cassino before moving to the University of Naples as a young teenager. That move proved decisive for Aquinas as it was in Naples that he was exposed to the works of Aristotle, whose ideas came to influence him deeply. Despite strong opposition from his family, at the age of 19 or 20, Aquinas eventually joined the Dominican order and after a few years at the University of Paris he studied in Cologne under Albert the Great from 1248 to 1252. Aquinas' major writings started with a treatise on Peter Lombard's *Sentences* – by then a standard work in higher education – and culminated with the highly influential *Summa Theologica*, which eventually came to replace Lombard's book as the major reference in theology and philosophy and remains one of key texts in these fields to this day.[2] The influence of Aquinas is well summarized by Rothbard (2006, p. 51) when he describes him as 'the towering intellect of the High Middle Ages, the man who built on the philosophical system of Aristotle, on the concept of natural law, and on Christian theology to forge "Thomism", a mighty synthesis of philosophy, theology and the sciences of man'. Aquinas authored commentaries on biblical texts, Aristotle, and other relevant authors, as well as textbooks and numerous interventions on theoretical controversies and current issues of his time. His writings comprise over eight million words, averaging the amazing mark of over 1,000 words a day, every day for two decades.[3]

The key distinguishing feature of Aquinas' thought is often identified as his attempt to fuse and redevelop Aristotelianism in a Christian framework, although his political philosophy combines Aristotelian elements with Platonic ones. Aquinas' political philosophy took Aristotle's teachings and interpreted them in light of the Bible and the earlier Christian tradition of political thought which already made use of Roman Law and elements of Platonic and Stoic philosophy.[4] The resulting mix proved particularly successful and appealing and so there are indeed good reasons to credit Aquinas with the merit of having contributed uniquely to build Aristotle's position as the leading figure in Western philosophy.

While Thomist thought came to be gradually attacked and laid aside in many Northern European universities from the fourteenth century onwards, in Iberia it did not subside and came to experience an unprecedented development and revival in the works of the late Iberian scholastics. While authors such as Vitoria, de Soto, Molina and Suárez differ in some aspects of their approaches to politics, they all share a solid adherence to Thomism, and particularly to the Thomist understanding of natural law and his typology of laws.[5]

For Aquinas, there are four types of law: eternal law, divine law, natural law and human law.[6] Eternal law is the most comprehensive notion of the four and essentially corresponds to the rational pattern in God's mind, which governs the entire universe. Being the most general of the four kinds of law, eternal law therefore includes a section related specifically with mankind and its relationship with the world: this natural law (*lex naturalis*), which can be apprehended by human reason. For Aquinas (and his followers) natural law is natural not in the sense of merely being instinctive to man as an animal but in the sense that man, as a rational being, is naturally able to distinguish right from wrong through the use of reason. As a substance, man shares with all substances an inclination towards preservation of his being according to his own nature; as an animal, man shares with other animals more specific ends, namely the inclination for the 'union of male and female and the education of the young and similar things'; as a rational creature, man has an additional natural inclination to employ reason in order to search for the truth about God and life in society.[7]

While natural law can be clearly understood through the correct employment of human reason, it does not supply more than general rules for human conduct and its precepts are often insufficient to serve as a guide for everyday actions. The more general moral principles are the ones that can be ascertained with a greater degree of certainty and by a larger number of people. The difficulties grow when man tries to understand more specific principles or apply general principles to concrete circumstances. Hence Aquinas also distinguishes between the primary precepts of natural law – common to all men at all times – and the secondary precepts of natural law – which differ according to varying circumstances and cannot be known and applied with the same degree of certitude as the primary precepts. The fact that natural law provides clear guidance only at a general level makes necessary the existence of human law. Life in society and the pursuit of the common good require that supplementary human laws be derived through a process of inference from the precepts of natural law. Human laws then can also be distinguished by their proximity to general principles of natural law: some laws are applied only to the specific circumstances of a given commonwealth and its rationale is only remotely connected with natural law, whereas other human laws tend to be shared by all peoples because they are very close reflections of the general principles of natural law.[8]

All human laws must derive, however indirectly, from the general principles of natural law, which are common to all mankind and always binding but human laws must additionally respond to the particular demands of time and place and are therefore apt to be changed in order to adapt to circumstances. But what if 'laws' that are not in accordance with natural law are imposed on a commonwealth? For Aquinas (as well as those in the Thomist tradition), these unjust 'laws' are in fact not laws at all and so cannot command a duty to be obeyed. Aquinas' theory of law can also be described as 'intellectualist', in the sense that the moral content of law is derived from its accordance with rational standards and not from the 'voluntarist' command expressing the legislator's will.[9] It is in the context of this intellectualist approach that Aquinas declares that legislation which is contrary to natural law as it can be apprehended by reason should not in fact be regarded as law at all.

Even though unjust laws should be obeyed if the consequences of disobedience are expected to be worse than those of complying with it, it does not bind its subjects in conscience. The Thomist emphasis on the idea that the ability of positive human laws to command obedience is dependent on their compliance with the general principles of natural law and not on their being an expression of the will of the ruler is particularly prevalent in the many of the works of the late Iberian scholastics.

The fourth kind of law in the Thomist framework is divine law, which has the particularity of not being derived through the employment of human reason but instead resulting from revelation through biblical texts and the Church. Whereas human law deals with life in society and the demands of a just political order, divine law is primarily concerned with the prospects for eternal salvation. Broadly speaking, in the Thomist framework, divine law addresses essentially the religious requirements necessary for one's salvation while human law is expected to deal with civic matters.

The distinction between divine law and human law echoes a broader Thomist concern to clearly articulate the distinct roles of faith and reason. For Aquinas, theology and philosophy are distinct sciences. Philosophy deals with the employment of reason and self-evident principles to study the natural order of the universe and to comprehend the laws that govern it. Theology deals with employing reason to understand the implications of (divinely) revealed knowledge. Whereas philosophy starts from self-evident principles and does not require the acceptance of divine grace, the foundations of theology lay in knowledge that presupposes faith. This approach to the relationship between philosophy and theology assumes a deep-rooted compatibility between divine grace and nature. Revealed knowledge and knowledge obtained exclusively through rational and empirical means are recognized as separate but they are also held to be fundamentally compatible. Divine grace is not in opposition to nature and in fact is regarded as having the potential to perfect nature and allowing it to rise to serve a higher purpose.[10]

The essence of the Thomist tradition in articulating moral theology, natural law and reason lies in the attempt to provide a rational foundation for ethics that can be accepted by thinking human beings independently of their faith. For Aquinas, while divine revelation and grace provide guidance and are important for eternal salvation, human law does not derive from divine law but from natural law which is accessible through the employment of 'right reason'.[11]

### The European revival of Thomism and the Salamanca School

The sixteenth-century renewal of scholasticism – giving rise to the late scholastic movement that would be active well into the seventeenth century and in which the Salamanca scholars played a central role – is largely coincident with the European revival of Thomism. At many important Universities, Peter Lombard's *Sentences* was gradually replaced by Thomas Aquinas' *Summa Theologica* as the main work to be studied, a shift that largely coincided with a renewal of the curricula away from the strict forms of nominalism[12] that had become dominant.[13] A crucial moment took place at the University of Paris in the first decade of the sixteenth century, when Pierre Crockaert (c. 1450–1514) started to lecture primarily on Aquinas instead of Lombard.[14] Almost simultaneously, the influential Dominican Thomas de Vio (1469–1534) – often referred to as Cardinal Cajetan – was also writing and lecturing on Aquinas in Italy while others spearheaded the Thomist renewal in Germany and in Spanish Universities like Seville and Alcalá. Cajetan was a particularly influential figure in the Thomist revival since his commentaries on St Thomas' *Summa* (published between 1514 and 1519) positioned him as a standard authority on the matter for centuries to come.[15]

However, not withstanding the significance of Cajetan's influence, the most important event in the consolidation of this European movement of renewed interest in Thomism was probably the appointment of Francisco de Vitoria – who had been a student of Crockaert in Paris – to the prime chair of theology at the University of Salamanca. Some of the most important first steps of the Thomist revival took place in Italy and in France but the movement was to be definitely carried forth and greatly expanded by the late Iberian scholastics.[16] The founder of the Salamanca School is often credited as the intellectual leader of the Thomist renewal movement and there are good reasons for that, since, despite some nominalist influences, Vitoria followed in most important points the fundamental tenets of Aquinas' teachings. The Thomist theory of natural law had a particular strong and lasting influence in Vitoria, whose intellectualist (rather than voluntarist) approach to law bears the clear imprint of Aquinas (an imprint that is even stronger in Domingo de Soto). Upon assuming his position at Salamanca, Vitoria was faced with the statutory obligation of teaching Lombard's *Sentences*, but decided not to accept the status quo and so he persisted until he was finally allowed to lecture primarily on Aquinas. He started by trying to redesign his lectures in a way that allowed him to comment simultaneously on Aquinas, but when the new statutes of 1538 restated the obligation of using Lombard's *Sentences* Vitoria eventually suffered a breakdown from the efforts of attempting to comment on both at the same time. He was then unofficially given permission by the University of Salamanca to comment exclusively on Aquinas' *Summa Theologica* and the authorization was eventually made official in 1550. In 1561, Vitoria's approach was made the general rule, with Aquinas assuming the role of main reference and reference being made only to select passages of Lombard.[17]

Given the University of Salamanca's prominence and growing influence at the time, the gradual affirmation of Thomism there is to a considerable extent representative of the wider trend that would persist well into the seventeenth century.

The persisting importance of the Thomist framework for the Salamanca School is also evident in later Jesuit authors, such as the influential Francisco Suárez. In the prefaces to his works, Suárez repeatedly assures the reader of his wish to be a faithful follower of Aquinas and proclaims his utmost respect and admiration for his teachings. Suárez was a strong proponent of the authority of Aquinas and was influential in widening the reach of Thomism both generally and particularly among Jesuit scholars.[18] Even though Suárez does on some important issues (both theological and philosophical) deviate from Aquinas, he attempts to do so only after careful consideration of preceding Thomist commentaries. For the most part, Suárez' contributions on political matters remain under the form of discussions and reflections on Thomist teachings and this is a feature that is characteristic of a large number (although not all) of the more relevant works of the Salamanca School.

In the context – and to a large extent in the leading role – of the European revival of Thomism, the authors of the Salamanca School incorporated many of Aquinas key points in the development of their own political ideas. While it would be impossible to list every one of them in detail and to consider in depth differences between the approaches of the distinct late Iberian scholastics, it's nevertheless possible to outline what were arguably the main Thomist inputs taken onboard by the Salamanca School.

First, despite the strong and undeniable emphasis on objective right and the common good, the Thomist framework, through its strong affirmation of the precedence of natural law over positive law, provided a strong basis upon which a defence of individual rights could later be developed. In fact, contrary to popular misconceptions about the Middle Ages, there are numerous stances of the affirmation of ideas favourable to individual rights in core medieval political theory. The protection accrued to acquired rights was dependent upon the firmness of their connection to natural law but rights held to be directly derived from natural law (such as the right to defend one's life) were often granted absolute supremacy over positive law. Although the explicit treatment of individual rights would only come significantly later – a development in which the Salamanca School played a crucial role – the Thomist natural law framework provided fertile ground for such ideas to be worked out.[19]

It was also this strong emphasis on natural law and the Thomist hierarchy of laws that led the late Iberian scholastics to explicitly address a number of political questions by reference to a supra-political moral standard.[20] In other words, the Thomist framework provided important intellectual arguments to judge the actions of even the most powerful political rulers by common moral and ethical standards. Positive law was not deemed enough to justify a given political stance, since both political decision-makers and the positive laws themselves were held to be liable before the general precepts of natural law. In addition to providing a basis for the later development of natural law theories of individual rights, the Thomist tradition – at least in the way it was developed by the Salamanca School – also allowed positive laws to be judged against the general and higher standard of natural law, which not even the mightiest emperor might legitimately declare himself exempt from the obligation of respecting.

The Thomist idea that natural law could be accessed and understood through the employment of human reason also came to be an important foundation for the political thought of the Salamanca School, both at a theoretical and at an applied level. The notion that the ability to discover and understand the principles of natural law and justice was not dependent on faith or on revealed knowledge proved a powerful one when explored in depth, but the rationale was in fact relatively straightforward. As laid out by Skinner (1978, p. 151):

> . . . since the law of nature is also right reason, we do not need to have any knowledge of revelation or divine positive law in order to be able to grasp and follow its essential principles. The law of nature is in short made known to men simply as men. This contention is presented by all these writers in the form of an appeal, with only minor variations, to the same cluster of metaphors.[21]

The commonly employed metaphor consisted in regarding the principles of natural law as being deeply embedded (even if not immediately accessible) in the structure of the human mind. It was this conception that underwrote the position that natural law could be both understood and justified through the sole use of human reason without recourse to (and without being dependent upon) revealed knowledge.

An additional element of the Thomist framework that was greatly influential for the Salamanca School was Aquinas' views on tyranny. Whereas in the traditional Augustinian perspective, tyranny was to be regarded essentially as a punishment for mankind's sinful condition and the scope for legitimate disobedience was very limited, Thomism has a wider potential role for active resistance to political rulers who behave in a tyrannical fashion. Since political rulers have a duty to respect natural law and promote the common good, the grave neglect of these functions may break the obligation of obedience and even lead to legitimate resistance by the people.[22] Although Aquinas does not put forth in detail the circumstances that legitimate active resistance and the processes through which such acts are to take place, the Thomist perspectives on the topic were one of the main influences for the theories developed by the late Iberian scholastics.

In the context of the European revival of Thomism, a final note should be stressed about economy, since this was one of the areas where the Salamanca School provided more key contributions. In this domain, although the Thomist framework never ceases to be a point of reference, the late Iberian scholastics that provided the most significant contributions to political economy did so in several instances either by resolving ambiguities present in Aquinas (which in many cases had their roots in Aristotle) or by going beyond the Thomist framework. In this sense, the political philosophy of the Salamanca School can be regarded as a more direct heir of Aquinas than the political economy, which on some key topics introduced more radical innovations on their Thomist predecessors.[23]

**Theological-political disputes**

The Thomist framework – and particularly its outlook on natural law and the nature of political society – clearly played a structuring role in many of the ideas of the Salamanca School but there was another great source of doctrinal influence: the crucial theological-political disputes that took place immediately before or were contemporary to the lives of the late Iberian scholastics.

First and foremost among these were of course the Protestant Reformation movement and the Catholic Counter-Reformation that ensued.[24] The Protestant challenge to the Roman Catholic Church has traditionally been symbolically associated with the 1517 posting of the Ninety-Five Theses – the articles which represent Martin Luther's attack on the established Church. Luther's own spiritual motivations were focused on the perceived need to go back to a supposed purer reading of the scriptures that broke away from the corrupt interpretations and misuses added throughout the times. This motivation quite directly led him to confront both the internal and external powers of the Church and put into question the established answers to central theological questions such as the role of divine grace in salvation.[25]

Approaching the issue through the less spiritually focused lenses of the 'economics of religion' in an analysis that greatly over-simplifies but nevertheless provides an interesting viewpoint, Ekelund et al. (2006, p. viii) describe the Protestant Reformation as an assault on the market leadership of the Catholic Church and the Counter-Reformation as a competitive reaction, with both movements fostering 'doctrinal and organizational innovations'.

Regardless of the more temporal or spiritual approach taken to the analysis of the Reformation and Counter-Reformation, both movements can only be understood in the context of the difficulties and pre-Reformation reform efforts of the medieval Church.[26] In the decades that preceded the Protestant break-up administrative, educational, disciplinary and moral problems mounted in the Catholic hierarchies and the Curia. This led to several reform initiatives but – partly due to internal power disputes – reform efforts had little impact. The Fifth Lateran Council, convened in Rome in 1512, was the last major effort at internal reform before the Protestant Reformation eventually came to materialize but, despite indisputable conscience of the existing problems, the Council proved insufficient to stem the latent Protestant movement.

The Protestant Reformation initially made the enactment of reform initiatives within the Roman Catholic Church even harder. If internal reform was already hard before, after the Reformation it became even more so, since internal criticism was easily linked to Protestant sympathies, and Protestant propagandists were eager and quick to make use of Catholic criticism of the Church as evidence of the justice of their cause.[27]

After a series of attempts in the late 1530s and early 1540s to reconcile Catholics and Protestants eventually failed, the prospect of a deeply divided Christendom in Western and Central Europe became a reality. The Council of Trent (stretching from the mid-1540s to the 1560s in three main sessions) enacted important administrative reforms (particularly the enlargement of the power and autonomy of the bishops) but it also marked the definite rejection of all the major theological and doctrinal claims of Protestants.[28] In response to the Protestant-proclaimed reliance on the sole authority of the biblical texts, the Roman Catholic Church reaffirmed the joint authority of both the Bible and the Church's tradition, in the form of past decisions of popes and councils. Catholic doctrinal positions on the Mass, the sacraments, indulgences and the worshipping of saints were also strongly reaffirmed against Protestant claims. In this regard, the issue of salvation and its relationship with divine grace and free will is particularly telling, not only because it was arguably the most important doctrinal divergence but also because of the symbolic character it acquired in the theological-political disputations between Catholics and Protestants. Catholic doctrine had traditionally emphasized the role of righteous conduct and good works – freely chosen by man – in salvation whereas Luther made it clear that divine grace alone was to be invoked in this regard. The doctrine of 'double justification' had been put forth by several authors (including the humanist Erasmus) as an attempt to achieve a compromise between the two antagonistic positions by stressing that both divinely attributed grace and human works played a role in salvation. But 'double justification' as it was being formulated eventually proved incapable of solving the dispute, at least partly because of Luther's peculiarly extreme interpretation of Augustine's doctrine of original sin and his division of mankind into two irrevocably separated groups: the true Christians in a 'kingdom of God' and all other human beings in a 'kingdom of Satan'. Each human being was allocated to one of the two kingdoms and no third possibility exists, with the result being a perpetual and unavoidable conflict between the two until the Day of Judgement when Christ is to return.[29] The Council of Trent rejected salvation by grace alone through faith and 'reaffirmed the traditional view that faith formed by works of love saved people, salvation coming to man on the basis of an acquired, inherent righteousness, not an imputed, alien righteousness'.[30]

The widely perceived Catholic need to renew and reinvigorate the educational and doctrinal capabilities of both the clergy and the laity in order to face the Protestant challenge led to an unprecedented mobilization of intellectual and organizational resources. The best and most significant example of this feature of the Counter-Reformation is undoubtedly the creation and extremely rapid expansion of the Society of Jesus, that ended up supplying most of the later members of the Salamanca School, including Molina, Mariana and Suárez. The early Jesuits and their remarkable organization were largely shaped by the image, charisma and personal experience of Ignatius of Loyola (1491–1556), the founder of the Society of Jesus. Initially a soldier of the king, Ignatius went through a long process of spiritual transformation while he was recovering from severe wounds inflicted to him in the battlefield. The key elements of Ignatius' peculiar spiritual approach are expressed in his *Spiritual Exercises*, which became a true mystical and psychological guide for the Society of Jesus prescribing a rigorous programme for physical and mental self-discipline and for the control and redirection of basic human emotions and the mind's faculties.[31] In a way, as emphasized by Ozment (1980, p. 412), the contrast between Martin Luther – the initiator and leader of the Protestant Reformation – and Ignatius of Loyola – the founder of the Catholic organization that assumed the leading role in the Counter-Reformation – summarizes much of what was at stake in the intense theological-political disputes of the period:

> In the persons of their founders the antithetical character of original Protestant and Counter Reformation piety is strikingly revealed. Whereas Luther had despaired of calculated efforts at self-reform and salvation, concluding that neither sublimation nor repression, no matter how diligently practiced, could ever bring peace of mind, Ignatius carefully examined himself and discovered a self-control like that of the first man, who could sin or not sin at will. Here was a new type of religious self-confidence that ran counter not only to the Reformation, but to much traditional spirituality as well.

Officially recognized by Pope Paul III in 1540, the Society of Jesus was initially restricted by Rome to a maximum of just 60 members and its original documents were far from anticipating the decisive role the Jesuits would play in the coming decades, particularly in the educational and intellectual domains.[32] The initial aims of the Society of Jesus pointed mainly to missionary work, but the rigorous self-discipline of the highly educated and uniquely motivated early Jesuits also soon made them coveted as confessors, advisors and educators.[33] With the added pressure of the Catholic need to supply answers and refutations to the Protestant challenges, it took only a few years for Jesuit scholars to assume a leading role in theological, philosophical and political discussions of the time.[34]

Not withstanding other ponderous reasons of a theoretical and philosophical nature, it's very likely that the conditions generated by the theological and political disputes of their time fostered in the late Iberian scholastics an even greater sensitivity to the abuses of political power. The scholastic tradition in which the Salamanca School had its roots had always tended to emphasize that natural law was prior and superior to any existing political order, that governments must pursue the common good and that obedience to political rulers is not unconditional. The existing political and religious conditions in the sixteenth and seventeenth century must often have had the effect of reinforcing in the minds of the late Iberian scholastics the need to place the power of the state within its proper boundaries and to reaffirm the autonomy of ecclesiastical power and the limits of political authority. The European revival of Thomism and the theological-political disputes of the time should therefore be considered jointly as self-reinforcing influences in the political thought of the Salamanca School.

## Applied Political Thought

The authors of the Salamanca School provided important contributions to a wide range of areas of applied political thought. The focus of the following sections is to outline their key ideas on the most salient topics.

### Individual rights and the common good

The prevailing contemporary notions of individual rights in Western political philosophy would probably be regarded as awkward by the late scholastics of Salamanca but they have nevertheless provided important contributions in this field. Looking at the Salamancans' understandings of what we would now call 'individual rights' (or 'subjective rights') and their articulation with the broader concept of justice provides insights that are worthy not only for the comprehension of the history of ideas but also for contemporary debates on those very same topics. In fact some of the key tensions in the thought of the late scholastics on justice, the common good and the rights of the individual anticipate tensions that are central in contemporary debates between conservative and libertarian authors and schools of thought.

The first point to keep in mind when attempting to provide a general overview of the thought of the Iberian late scholastics on individual rights is that the definite nature of their positions in this field (assuming a common ground exists in their positions) continues to be a matter of controversy. The core issue in this controversy can be synthesized as that of ascertaining whether the Salamanca School represents a resurgence and development of a truly Aristotelian and Thomist framework centred on an 'objective right' conception of natural law or if the authors of the School were in fact closer to the notion of 'subject right' focused on rights as individual liberties or faculties that ultimately became one of the features of modernity.[35]

The tension between the perceived demands of 'objective right' (understood in the sense of justice and the common good) and respect for individual (subjective) rights is present from the very beginning of the School, in the works of Francisco de Vitoria, and developed in later authors.

The late Iberian scholastics held what can be called an organic view of political society, with the common good as its main overriding goal. This view is however strongly qualified by a general recognition that the binding character of natural law extends not only to individual subjects but also to positive law and to the rulers themselves. The result is a peculiar combination of a largely organic conception on the promotion of order and the common good with an emphasis on local and individual rights. The promotion of order is deemed a priority but this common goal coexists with a wide range of individual, family and local rights, which limit both the power of temporal and spiritual rulers and are seen as prevailing over unjust legislation.[36]

Despite its central importance for the definition of the legitimate scope of individual rights, the notion of common good was, however, for the most part, taken for granted and not subject to intense scrutiny. This can probably be attributed (at least partially) to the fact that the question 'what is the common good?'

was not usually a main topic of investigation in the Thomist tradition (Höpfl 2004, p. 283) which framed much of the thought of the Salamanca School on individual rights.

Nevertheless, the late scholastics strongly asserted that the original condition of individuals was one of natural liberty, independence and equality in the sense that no man was presumed to hold political power over another.[37] Perhaps the best way to understand the approach of the Salamanca School to individual rights is to bear in mind Gierke's (1987, p. 7) classical description of medieval political thought:

> Political Thought when it is genuinely medieval starts from the Whole, but ascribes an intrinsic value to every Partial Whole down to and including the Individual. If it holds out one hand to Antique Thought when it sets the Whole before the Parts, and the other hand to the Modern Theories of Natural Law when it proclaims the intrinsic and aboriginal rights of the Individual, its peculiar characteristic is that it sees the Universe as one articulated Whole and every Being – whether a Joint-Being (Community) or a Single-Being – as both a Part and a Whole: a Part determined by the final cause of the Universe, and a Whole with a final cause of its own.

Depending on how one looks at the perspectives of the late Iberian scholastics on individual rights they can be seen either as the last traditional Thomists or as proposing an account of personal autonomy and liberty that attempts to deal with the challenges of (what we now call) the Modern period without jeopardizing traditional Thomist notions of justice and the common good.

Perhaps the best example of this stance can be found in the works of Francisco de Vitoria, the founder of the Salamanca School. Vitoria combines a strong adherence to the traditional Thomist conception of objective right with a nuanced and in some ways innovative understanding of personal autonomy associated with a distinct sphere of individual freedom. As noted by

Brett (1997, pp. 132–134), this is particularly clear in Vitoria's discussion of hunting and homicide. Thus Vitoria explicitly objects to local lords enacting limitations on the people's liberty to hunt wild animals even if it is claimed that the limitations are in the interest of the subjects (e.g. by helping them not to waste their time), because he regards the general preservation of liberty as taking precedence over the private good in a setting such as this. The autonomous direction of each individual towards his conscientious perception of the good is seen by Vitoria as a liberty worth preserving even if from the perspective of an external political authority the real good is conceived differently and the person in question is judged to be in error. In a similar vein, when discussing the act of killing in self-defence, Vitoria rejects the notion that only public or divine authority can justify killing and asserts a crucial role for private authority and private responsibility. In other words, Vitoria regards individual rights as indispensable components of a well-ordered society and therefore rejects limiting the notion of right to the obligation of acting in accordance with the law or an the dictates of an external authority. Without neglecting the sense of objective right and political obligation, Vitoria's understanding of rights also includes the notion of a personal sphere of liberty that – while bound by natural law – relies primarily on the individual's authority and responsibility to use reason and freely decide his course of action in his particular circumstances.

Domingo de Soto built upon the teachings of Vitoria to further refine the conceptual relationship between natural law and natural right (understood in a sense that allowed for a significant degree of individual liberty). While the nuances in de Soto's writings on the topic are numerous and complex, it seems appropriate to state that his 'great achievement was to defend simultaneously the right of the city and the right of the individual man within it' (Brett 1997, p. 164).[38] De Soto's insistence on the intrinsic value of each individual is particularly clear in the following passage of *De iustitia et iure*, where de Soto makes a crucial distinction and a strong affirmation of that value in the context of discussing the impermissibility of killing an innocent:

> If someone threatened to kill me if I do not commit to cut one of my hands or my tongue, I could deliver that member [i.e. that part of the human body] in order to conserve my life, even though the cutting is only a necessary mean due to the malice of another [the one who makes the threat]; as a consequence, in the same way, a nation could deliver [i.e. sacrifice] one of its citizens. This consequence must be denied because a member [i.e. a part of the human body] has no distinct existence from the existence of the whole, nor in any way does it exist for itself, but for the whole; nor is it capable in itself of right or injustice. But a man, although he is part of the commonwealth, is nevertheless also a person existing for himself, and so capable of suffering injustice, which the commonwealth may not impose on him . . .[39]

The Jesuit members of the Salamanca School shared, for the most part (particularly Suárez, not as much Molina and even less pronouncedly Mariana), the rather wide conception of the common good in terms of the limitations on individual rights it entailed that was prevalent among Jesuit scholars of the time.[40] At the same time, however, the reasoning that led self-defence to be regarded as an indisputable natural right was grounded – as in Vitoria and de Soto – in the affirmation of a sphere of individual liberty and autonomy that was independent and above the legitimacy of positive law and the political power of rulers.[41] Not only was the conception of self-defence rather wide – extending to an individual's life, physical and moral integrity, and property as well as to the protection of unjustly aggressed third parties – it also included the notion – for example, for Molina – that the victim's fear was the primary standard by which the proportionality of the force employed in the act of self-defence was to be judged. Threats to property were generally regarded as extremely serious offences with the killing of thieves held to be a legitimate act of self-defence under several arguments (such as the implicit risk to one's life and integrity or the importance of property for self-preservation). More controversially, some of the late Iberian scholastics – with Mariana as the leading exponent of this view – went as far as explicitly affirming the right of an individual to legitimately kill political rulers who behaved as tyrants. Although the justification for property was regarded as deriving from the promotion of the common good (and not as an absolute natural right), the institution of private property tended to be strongly defended by the late scholastics. This defence tended to rely on quasi-utilitarian grounds, with justifications that appealed far more to arguments that property fostered the common good than to the affirmation of individual rights per se (unlike what happened in the case of individual rights to self-defence).[42]

The clearest (although not the most nuanced) overview of the perspective of the Salamanca School on individual rights can perhaps be obtained by considering the ideas of Diego de Covarrubias y Leyva on this topic.[43] Building upon the teachings of Vitoria and Azpilcueta, Covarrubias regarded the natural condition of men as one of equal freedom in a universal society. Even though human society constantly changes throughout history, each individual – with a shared and universal human nature – is regarded as a permanent member of mankind. From the conditions of this natural state of liberty and equality, Covarrubias derives a series of rights that are to be held as universally valid and inseparable from a proper understanding of the common good. These include individual rights to life, liberty and religion and rights that ought to be recognized by mankind as a universal society, such as property, peace and emigration. Covarrubias' understanding of fundamental rights overrides distinctions between historical circumstances and political regimes and this, at least in principle, meant they ought to be applied to all mankind. The state and the legitimate exercise of political power is, therefore, to be subordinated to the requirements of universal rights and the promotion of the common good.

In the same way that individual liberty is bound by natural law and must not lead to arbitrary acts, legitimate political power must not degenerate into absolutist or tyrannical forms. It is this dynamic and intertwined understanding of both the common good and individual rights that constitute the main limits on the extension and exercise of legitimate political power as understood by the late Iberian scholastics.

**The state and the limits of political power**

The political thought of the Salamanca School stood in firm opposition to absolutist positions and held very definite views on the necessary limits of political power. In this broad sense, they may certainly be considered as constitutionalist (or at least preconstitutionalist) authors even though may not necessarily be considered as such according to more technical and narrow definitions of these terms. The scholastic tradition which they furthered tended to either reject or strongly qualify the notion of a self-sustaining sovereignty of the ruler over and above the sovereignty of the people. In this tradition, the relationship between the citizens and the ruler is of a contractual or quasi-contractual nature, meaning that the exercise of political power is legitimate only if it respects the terms of the implied contract. The implications of this tradition in medieval political thought were stated in the maxim '*Populus maior principe*' and meant that whatever the form of government, there remained an element of popular sovereignty. It was upon this that rights of resistance to tyrants were generally recognized and that the idea that, at least in extreme circumstances, a ruler might be legitimately deposed was gradually developed.[44]

The development of these insights led to the development of the theories on tyrannicide and resistance to political power (analysed further below) but the contributions of the Salamanca School to the theory of the state go beyond that point.

It is worth remembering (and reinforcing) here that in the context of the Thomist framework within which the late Iberian scholastics largely operated, positive human laws are only held to be genuine laws to the extent they are in accordance (or at least do not violate) the general principles of natural law.[45] As can be readily seen, there lies a first – and very significant – limitation on the exercise of political power: unjust pieces of legislation (i.e. those which are in opposition to natural law) are not to be considered law and do not in themselves command obedience (though, depending on social circumstances and on the consequences of disobedience there may be other compelling reasons to obey them). Vitoria, for example, in his *relectione* on civil power (*De potestate civili*) grants that public power is from God in the sense that is founded upon natural law but then adds that 'the material cause on which this naturally and divinely appointed power rests is the commonwealth', which 'takes upon itself the task of governing and administering itself and directing all its powers to the common good'.[46]

The commonwealth delegates to political agents the authority to legislate but for Vitoria (1991, p. 12) it's clear who originally holds legislative power:

> . . . positive law derives from the commonwealth, and therefore the existence of the commonwealth itself and of its power to make laws must precede the existence of positive laws; consequently it may be deduced that this legislative power itself exists in the commonwealth by divine and natural law.

This process of delegation is of a secular nature and does not imply direct divine intervention in setting up governments. In fact, the idea that worldly governments are directly instituted by God was regarded as a dangerous heresy. As stressed by Skinner (1978, p. 154), the Thomists wished 'to claim that all secular commonwealths must originally have been set up by their own citizens as a means of fulfilling their purely mundane ends'. But here Vitoria faces an apparent difficulty for he appears to wish to continue affirming that the power of legitimate kings proceeds from God while simultaneously clearly pointing out that the original authority to legislate positive human law lies with the commonwealth, not the ruler.[47] The solution to this paradox comes from the distinction between *potestas* (power) and *auctoritas* (authority). If power is understood as the royal capability to rule, then it may be said that, like other human capabilities, it is an innate endowment derived from God. However, if we think about authority (understood as executive 'power'), then it lies originally with the commonwealth and is only exercised by the ruler upon delegation (even tough it may be a form of implicit and historically necessary delegation).[48]

That the political ruler, despite deriving his capability to rule from God, is conceived by Vitoria (1991, p. 14) as an agent of the commonwealth made necessary to solve perceived collective action problems is clear in the following passage:

> The commonwealth as such cannot frame laws, propose policies, judge disputes, punish transgressors, or generally impose its laws on the individual, and so it must necessarily entrust all this business to a single man.

To Vitoria, the political ruler does not therefore become in any way the 'owner' of the commonwealth: he merely receives (from the commonwealth) the authority to administrate collective affairs in accordance with the promotion of the common good. As stressed by Fernandéz-Santamaria (1977, p. 74), 'the prince is the nation's minister and caretaker; to rule means to fulfil the obligations implicit in the commonwealth's trust.'

In the original condition or state of nature, however, there was no political power to be found and all men were free and equal.[49] Man is a social animal that requires life in community both to better face the hazards of nature (making up for his individual physical limitations) and to flourish fully, since justice and friendship can only be practised and experienced by living in society with other persons. But political society does not derive directly from the social inclinations of man. Rather, the emergence of the state is explained by historical circumstances and not rooted directly in natural law. This leads to a tension in

Vitoria's thought since the politically organized commonwealth cannot be grounded on strict natural law grounds (man was, after all, born free and no man held political power over another in the state of nature) but the coercive apparatus of the state is nevertheless affirmed as necessary to preserve human society in present historical circumstances.[50] Political power provides a solution to specific human needs – and to that extent it is not in contradiction with natural law – but the justification for the existence of the state must be sought in history and not directly in the general principles of natural law. From the perspective of natural law, both (hypothetical) pre-political and political societies are held by Vitoria to be in a somewhat similar position. Both are consonant with natural law but apply to different contexts and answer different needs. In pre-historical society, the state's coercive power was not necessary but the conduct and requirements of actual historical man impose the establishment of political organization. This means that political power is affirmed as necessary in actual history but also that both the state and positive human law are only justified in so far as they contribute to the fulfilment of natural law.

In the process of arguing in favour of monarchy as the best form of government Vitoria (1991) provides another crucial insight about the relationship between liberty and political regimes. He starts by asserting that the claims of enjoying greater liberty by democratic 'civil societies' are unfounded (p. 19):

> Civil societies which have no sovereign and are ruled by a popular administration often boast of their liberty, accusing other civil societies of being the servile bondsmen of sovereigns. There are even some within this kingdom who subscribe to this view.
>
> Against this stupid and ignorant idea I offer my first corollary, which is that *there is no less liberty under a monarchy than under an aristocracy or timocracy* [rule of the multitude].

And Vitoria (1991, p. 20) proceeds to justify his position on terms that show a sophisticated understanding of the distinction between the form of government and the way political power is exercised:

> I demonstrate the major premiss from what has been said already: under any type of government, each private individual is subject to the public power, which he is bound to obey, whether that power resides in one man or in a number of men or in the whole multitude. This power is the same, whether it be exercised by one man, or by the whole community or commonwealth, or by the nobles; there is clearly no greater liberty in being subject to three hundred senators than to one king. Indeed, men who are subject to the decree and government of the crowd have, by that token, all the more masters – unless anyone is so mad as to believe himself a slave when he obeys one wise king, and fancy himself free when he is subject to a barbarous mob.

This theoretical conception of the state is markedly distinct from absolutist and patriarchalist approaches but leaves two important questions insufficiently answered. The first is what the specific historical motivations may have been for men to give up their original condition of freedom. The second is about the conditions under which the establishment of political power may be regarded as legitimate. While Vitoria and his contemporary Dominican scholastics did not provide full and complete answers to these questions, the later Jesuit members of the Salamanca School would further develop ideas in this regard.[51] Both Molina and Suárez suggest that the primary motivations for the establishment of political power flow from the recognition of the risks of injustice and uncertainty associated with man's fallen nature.[52] While they do not discard the Thomist framework about human nature (they still consider man to be capable of perceiving the general principles of natural law) Molina and (even more so) Suárez share a substantially pessimistic view of human conduct in the absence of coercive enforcement of positive laws. Natural liberty is thus rationally 'traded' for the added security and stability that the establishment of a public authority can provide. As for the second question, the key to judging the legitimacy of the establishment of the state lies in the idea of popular consent.[53] This consent is founded upon the rational recognition of the need to enact a state in order to promote order and justice, and better safeguard security, liberties and property. The legitimate enactment of a state endowed with coercive power is thus founded upon the rational (even if only tacit) consent that grows from the comprehension of the necessity of abandoning the conditions of natural liberty.[54]

Among the main authors of the Salamanca School, Suárez was possibly the one who most emphasized the congruence of political power with natural law. Even though he clearly asserted that men were born free and therefore not subject to the sovereignty of any human ruler, Suárez emphasized that men were also born potentially subject to political power. Given that historical reality and the sinful condition of man, the state cannot be said to be in contradiction with natural law, even though it is not directly instituted by natural law. Suárez also developed at some length the process through which the commonwealth as a whole might legitimately institute a particular regime. For this end, Suárez employed explicitly contractual terms to describe how political authority emanates from a choice on the part of the people.[55] Although in some instances Suárez makes use of tacit forms of consent, more often than not he associates consent with a very concrete contractual agreement or pact (*pactum*) through which the commonwealth congregated as a whole both transfers political authority and gives rise to a genuine political community.

Suárez' conception of the *pactum* logically lends support to affirming the existence of limits on political authority and this was also how the theories of the early Jesuits tended to be perceived at their time.[56] Interpretations which place Suárez as a precursor to absolutism are therefore very hard to support.[57] Suárez' *Defensio fidei* – with strong arguments on favour of individual and communal rights of self-defence against the abuses of political power – is a clear statement of his opposition to royal absolutism and it was in fact widely perceived as such at the time.[58]

To the (limited) extent the Salamanca School can be taken as a whole on this topic, it's possible to state that even if tacit primordial consent was held to be sufficient, the widespread and consistent emphasis on the role of consent in the establishment of political power implicitly strengthened the notion that there were limits to government. Limits which also justified that – at least in extreme circumstances and when no other workable options were available – the people could legitimately resist and even depose and kill tyrannical political rulers.

**Legitimate resistance and tyrannicide**

The issues of legitimate resistance and tyrannicide were – understandably – two of the most controversial problems of the time. First, because they obviously risked jeopardizing the stability of existing political structures and trigger the anger of rulers; and second because the discussion necessarily involved the problematic distinction between regicide (the unlawful and on all accounts undesirable killing of a legitimate monarch) and tyrannicide (the killing of a tyrant, an act which might be justified under some circumstances). It therefore should not come as a surprise that even among authors broadly associated within the Salamanca School positions on this issue were not unanimous.

The common thread of the prevailing view was that rulers abusing their power in a tyrannical fashion could be deposed and even killed but only if the offences against the common good were sufficiently grave and if it was done through a valid judicial process. The judicial procedure, however, tended to be identified in strong terms as a requirement but was only vaguely defined, particularly in terms of defining who was supposed to have the final decision on the judgement in order for it to be considered valid. The requirement of grave violations against the common good essentially meant that given the risk of generating strife, disorder and civil war, the option of tyrannicide should by no means be taken lightly but only under fairly extreme circumstances.

The affirmative but nevertheless reluctant attitude towards the possibility of legitimately deposing and even killing a tyrant is best exemplified in Vitoria (1991, p. 200), when he states that although the commonwealth cannot reclaim its authority from a legitimate monarch if it has 'transferred it unconditionally and in perpetuity to the king and its successors', it nevertheless retains by natural law a right to resist and if necessary depose a tyrannical ruler:

> ... it remains true that if a king proves to be a tyrant in government the commonwealth can depose him, because even if the commonwealth has given away its authority it keeps its natural right to defend itself; if there is no other way, it may reject its king.

The imprecise definition of the conditions under which resistance would become legitimate and the process through which they could be determined obviously generated a practical tension between the general duty to obey legitimate authorities and the right to resist tyranny. Later authors of the Salamanca School would (in most cases cautiously) contribute to reduce this tension by elaborating on these topics. The Jesuit Suárez provides in his *Defensio fidei* a relatively clear and explicit description of the conditions for legitimate resistance and argues that tyrannicide is justified if it is

> essential for the liberty, because if there is any less drastic means of removing him it is not lawful to kill him forthwith without the approval of a superior and an investigation. This includes the proviso that no treaty, truce or pact ratified under oath has been made between the tyrant and the people. . . . For pacts and oaths, even those made with enemies, must be kept unless they are clearly unjust and extorted by force. We must add still another restriction; always provided that there

is no danger of the same or worse evils falling on the community as a result of the tyrant's death as it already suffers under his rule.[59]

While Suárez takes great care to set boundaries and conditions for legitimate resistance against political rulers, he undoubtedly affirms – through an analogy between individual rights and the rights of the commonwealth – that the concept of self-defence also applies against kings.[60] No *pactum* may remove the right to self-preservation and so, in extreme conditions and provided that the decision is taken by an assembly that properly represents the commonwealth, it is possible to legitimately depose and even kill a political ruler. Additionally, if the tyranny is manifest – as is the case when the ruler is an usurper (i.e. holds his position illegitimately) – tacit consent by the commonwealth is assumed and sufficient to legitimately kill the tyrant. And even the distinction between legitimate and illegitimate rulers is not absolute since if a legitimate king is duly deposed he consequently becomes an illegitimate ruler, and therefore subject to being treated by the commonwealth as an usurper.[61]

Not withstanding Suárez' contributions, the clearest and most famous (or infamous, depending on one's views on the subject) treatment of legitimate resistance and tyrannicide among the late Iberian scholastics originated from another Jesuit: Juan de Mariana. In his highly controversial writings on the topic, Mariana emphasizes the role of direct popular (and even individual) resistance to the abuses of political power over more conventional (some could call them constitutional) constraints. Given the fallen condition of men, Mariana argues that laws are ultimately protected by the sentiments of fear imposed by the credible threat of sanctions in case they are violated. Mariana adds (in a way that can be seen as anticipating the logic of contemporary arguments in public choice theory) that this logic applies not only to subjects but also to rulers, since they are, after all, also men and therefore responsive to human motivations and fears. There is, however, an additional difficulty in attempting to enforce the law upon a tyrant: given their position of power, tyrants will not in most instances be in a position where the judicial system or other constitutional constraints exert a credible threat. The solution provided by Mariana is to establish the threat of assassination as a sort of para-constitutional constraint that may be effective in instilling some respect for the law upon political rulers.[62]

For Mariana, prudence dictates that the ruler should foster by his own example respect for the law and virtuous conduct among the general population, but this prudence is ultimately determined by the fear of the direct and personal consequences that may result from the undermining of the prince's legitimacy. The assassination of Henry III of France (1574–1589) is portrayed – controversially – as a result of the violation of the pragmatic rules of political prudence but the broader point involved in Mariana's discussion of tyrannicide is that the ultimate source of political authority resides with the people of the commonwealth and not in the person of the ruler himself, with the threat of assassination functioning as a necessary reminder of that principle. The full intended effect of the threat of tyrannicide is clear in the following passage by Mariana:

> It is a salutary reflection that princes have been persuaded that if they oppress the state, if they are unbearable on account of their vices and foulness, their position is such that they can be killed not only justly but with praise and glory. Perhaps this fear will give some pause lest they deliver themselves up to be deeply corrupted by vice and flattery; it will put reins on madness. This is the main point: that the prince should be persuaded that the authority of the commonwealth as a whole is greater than that of one man alone.[63]

When compared to other late Iberian scholastics, Mariana is somewhat more extreme in his presentation of the case for legitimate resistance and tyrannicide and he also departs to a large extent from the traditional Aristotelian-Thomist framework, preferring instead to reason from a pessimistic account of human nature and to give prominence to self-preservation. But it would be a mistake to completely isolate him from the rest of the authors of the Salamanca School in this regard. Mariana differed more in presentation and in the motives invoked than on the general conclusions about legitimate resistance and tyrannicide.[64]

**Church and state**

On matters of religion, the late Iberian scholastics generally subscribed to the traditionally held view that unity of the faith was an important value to preserve. The rationale for this widely shared position consisted in recognizing not only the personal importance of holding the (true) faith but also in the connection between religious observance and civic virtues.[65] Religious uniformity in Catholic kingdoms was generally defended both on spiritual and on secular grounds, to the extent that political stability and the common good of the commonwealth were held to be fostered by unity in observing the 'true religion' while the existence of religiously motivated political factions endangered the kingdom. This may present itself as an awkward position for contemporary readers, but it is worth bearing in mind that by the late seventeenth century, the celebrated Locke himself – in his *Letter Concerning Toleration* – explicitly denied toleration to atheists and to the Roman Catholic Church.[66]

Also in tune with the prevailing views of the time, the late Iberian scholastics established for the most part a significant distinction between pagans and heretics. There was general agreement within the Salamanca School that individuals who had never been Christians should not be compelled to become so. As for heretics, the prevailing opinion was that they could, at least in some circumstances, be forced to return to the true faith they had previously accepted.[67]

At the same time, however, there was on some topics a strong and growing emphasis on the importance of freedom and voluntary choice. It is worth noting, for example, the way in which Vitoria (1991, pp. 49–50) argues against attempts to prove that heretics are nevertheless still members of the Church:

> In conclusion, the word 'church' seems to mean nothing other than *the Christian commonwealth and religion*. It is of little importance, then, what theoretical rights or reasons are adduced to show that heretics are members of the Church, since their actions are in practice incompatible with membership of the Church. Deserters cannot be part of the army from which they deserted.
>
> In this relection, therefore, I use the term 'church' to mean only *the community or commonwealth of the faithful*.

Vitoria also came out firmly against the baptism of pagan children without parental consent.[68] Through valid baptism, a person becomes a member of the Church, but if the parents (who are primarily responsible for the education of their children) do not consent how can the child be brought up as a Christian? For Vitoria, overriding parental consent – even if for such an important matter as baptism – was a violation of natural law, which protects parental rights. Vitoria's opposition to baptizing children without parental concern extends even to the sons of slaves since slavery cannot be extended to spiritual matters.

The Jesuit scholastics were the most emphatic in asserting the value of religious unity but the circumstances of their time – particularly the Protestant Reformation – also led them to gradually develop progressively stronger qualifications to policies of religious intolerance and coercion towards heretics. While fighting heresy was deemed an indisputable duty, toleration might be justified by avoiding greater evils.[69] In other words, the necessity imposed by the specific circumstances of the time was gradually regarded as a possible legitimate justification even for the toleration of heresy.

The perceived challenges of heretics also played an important role in the definition of the doctrines of the late Iberian scholastics about the proper relationship between civil and religious authorities. As pointed out by Skinner (1978, p. 144):

> Confronted on all sides by 'the heretics of the age', the Dominican and Jesuit theorists reached back to the doctrines of the *via antiqua*, using them as a basis for developing a new, systematic and self-consciously orthodox view of the Church and its proper relationship with the secular commonwealth.

As for the late Iberian scholastics' view of the Church, they affirmed it as a visible institution founded by Christ, embodying a set of traditional doctrines and practices, holding jurisdictional powers on certain matters and united under the authority of the pope. On the dispute between 'papalist' (emphasizing the role and authority of the pope) and 'conciliarist' (emphasizing the role and authority of the councils as assemblies of ecclesiastical powers) visions of the Church, the School of Salamanca generally leaned towards affirming papal power against the perceived heresies of modernists. The papalist emphasis was more pronounced in later Jesuit authors such as Suárez, but Vitoria's own writings on the political and jurisdictional organization and powers of the Church devote substantial attention to the refutation of the positions of conciliarists such as Jean Gerson, John Mair and Jacques Almain.[70] At the same time, however, Vitoria accepted some of the premises of the conciliarists and avoided direct comparisons between the powers and relative position of the pope and of the councils.[71] Vitoria was also clear in asserting that the pope was bound by the directive force of laws (including even the ones he had made) and – following Cajetan – that there existed a (collective) right (and an obligation) to resist a pope whose actions were publicly, clearly and gravely ruining the Church.[72] In extreme cases, the pope might even be deposed through a legitimate jurisdictional process on grounds of heresy or madness.

The late Iberian scholastics also held firm views about the proper boundaries and separation between civil and religious powers. Building upon a basically Thomist framework, the independence and autonomy of secular power in its proper order (*in suo ordine*) was affirmed and positions arguing for the direct intervention of religious authorities on temporal matters were rejected.[73] Vitoria (1991, p. 88) rejects the notion that the pope has temporal power and draws a clear distinction:

Civil and temporal power is that which has a temporal end; spiritual power is that which has a spiritual end. I mean, then, that the pope has no power which is ordered to a temporal end, which is merely temporal power.

Unlike what happens with the clergy, secular authorities do not derive their temporal power from the pope nor are they subject to him on temporal matters. The pope possesses no temporal powers through which he could alter civil laws, interfere in non-spiritual matters related to civil government or depose secular rulers.[74]

The Jesuit Mariana, whose main concern may indeed be described as 'popular authority over the ruler' and not 'papal authority over kings',[75] is also particularly clear in rejecting outright any notion of 'papal absolutism' and in identifying the source of political power in the commonwealth, not the pope.[76] For Mariana, the heresy and misconduct of political rulers is to be dealt with through appropriate means by their subjects and not by the pope, who cannot depose secular authorities.

But perhaps the clearest view on this matter comes from the Dominican Domingo de Soto, as is eloquently summarized in the following passage from his *De iustitia et iure*:

> ... the civil power is not dependent upon the spiritual power in such a way that it is instituted by him, nor does it derive from him its virtue, nor may a king be deposed of its throne on account of him, nor forced, nor corrected, unless he breaks away from the divine laws and the spiritual end. Because even though both powers proceed from God, they do not however proceed one from the other, but through distinct ways: The first proceeds from God immediately, and the second from natural law and through society.[77]

The perspectives of the Salamanca School on the origin, organization and mutual relationship of civil and religious power led the late Iberian scholastics to affirm the legitimacy of pagan rulers and to state that they ought not to be deposed simply due to being pagan. Since temporal power does not proceed from spiritual power, there was in principle no reason why pagan rulers – just like Christian ones – might not be legitimate.[78] This is an insight that proved extremely important for the development of the late Iberian scholastics' theories of international law and for their analysis of issues related to the European colonization of America.

## International law and developments in Just War theory

Since the influence of the Salamanca School in the controversies concerning the New World is dealt with in the next chapter, this section seeks to present a brief overview of the main contributions of the late Iberian scholastics to international law and to Just War theory.

The origins of (what we now call) international law go back to the Roman law concept of *ius gentium*, a set of general principles and rules that are derived from natural reason (and not from national legislators), are common to all peoples, and apply equally to all mankind.[79] However, it was at the time of the Salamanca School that the consolidation of national states in Europe and the discovery of new politically organized communities in the East and in America provided an ideal context to explore some of the implications of a systematic approach to international law.[80]

Vitoria, Soto, Molina and Suárez all agreed that the *ius gentium* was common to all mankind and that it could be recognized by reason even though it was not created through the will of any assembly or human legislator. This law of nations included universally valid provisions for the basic rights to self-preservation, the institution of private property, diplomatic immunities and slavery as a form of safeguarding human lives in times of war.[81]

Other matters were more controversial, such as the freedom of commerce and the free movement and settlement of people. Vitoria was inclined to accept them as part of the *ius gentium* and even considered refusal of access as a just cause for war while Molina was critical of this position, arguing that a state may legitimately impose restrictions on the use of the country's common resources and possessions.[82]

Suárez elaborated on earlier contributions to provide in some respects a clearer picture of the *ius gentium* and international law. He divided the *ius gentium* into two categories: the first included domestic laws that were common to all (or most) states; the second involved laws that were common in the sense they applied to international interactions. Although both or were *ius gentium* in the sense they were very close to natural law and in principle applicable to all mankind, it is the second category (including, for example, the rules for international commerce, the rules of war and diplomatic immunities) that properly constitutes international law.[83] Suárez also emphasized the role of the *ius gentium* as the legal framework applicable to the universal community, a notion which is characteristic of the thought of the late Iberian scholastics but was not always as developed in previous works.

The *ius gentium*, with its universal applicability, therefore assumes the core role in the late Iberian scholastics' theory of international law. But since in this conception international law mostly assumes the form of unwritten law two additional questions arise: the first is about the binding force of the *ius gentium*; the second is about how to enforce it in practice.[84] Vitoria (1991, p. 21) is clear in affirming the binding force of the *ius gentium*, and associating it with a notion of (presumably tacit) consent by all mankind:

> The whole world, which is in a sense a commonwealth, has the power to enact laws which are just and convenient to all men; and these make up the law of nations. From this it follows that those who break the law of nations, whether in peace

or in war, are committing mortal crimes, at any rate in the case of graver transgressions such as violating the immunity of ambassadors. No kingdom may choose to ignore this law of nations, because it has the sanction of the whole world.

Suárez elaborated further on the customary character of the *ius gentium* and its independence both from formal agreements and from the specific legislative acts of nations but his main conclusions do not differ significantly from those of Vitoria.[85]

As for the coercive enforcement of international law, this is a question that leads directly to the late Iberian scholastics' perspectives on Just War.

Within the Salamanca School, the – so to speak – juridical function of war is perhaps more clearly synthesized in the works of Diego de Covarrubias, who puts forth a theory of Just War that diverges both from the pacifism characteristic of some humanist thought and from the more purely pragmatic approach of the Machiavellians.[86] For Covarrubias, war can only be justified if it aims at safeguarding the universal principles of the *ius gentium* in the international arena. The concept of Just War is thus inseparable from the notion of a just international order, which in turn depends upon respect for the principles of international law inscribed in the *ius gentium*. A just cause for war must therefore necessarily involve injury (or potential injury) resulting from a violation of the *ius gentium*. These injuries may be violations of natural law, of state-specific rights or of even of the rights of the universal community of peoples and legitimate war is conceived of as a coercive method to pursue justice. In this juridical conception of war, Covarrubias distinguishes essentially three forms of armed conflict. The first is defensive war (*bellum defensium*), with self-defence commonly regarded by all the late Iberian scholastics as an undisputable just cause for taking up arms against an aggressor.[87] For the state, self-defence includes taking direct action to recover property illegitimately and violently taken by an aggressor. The second is war aimed at the avenging of wrongs suffered (*bellum vindicatum*). Since there is no higher temporal authority to apply justice, for states the concept of self-defence leads to the possibility of vindicating the injuries suffered.[88] Additionally, the punishment of wrongdoers is also a just cause for armed conflict and corresponds to punitive war (*bellum punitium*). In practice, of course, all three types of war will tend to overlap in specific armed conflicts but the conceptual distinction is worth bearing in mind because the possibility of avenging wrongs and inflicting punishment is conceived both as a complement to self-defence and as a method of deterrence. Vitoria (1991, p. 300) is particularly explicit about this:

> The commonwealth, on the other hand, has the authority not only to defend itself, but also to avenge and punish injuries done to itself and its members. This is proved by Aristotle's dictum that 'the commonwealth should be self-sufficient (*sibi sufficiens*)'; the commonwealth cannot sufficiently guard the public good and its own stability unless it is able to avenge injuries and teach its enemies a lesson, since wrongdoers become bolder and readier to attack when they can do so without fear of punishment. So it is necessary for the proper administration of human affairs that this authority should be granted to the commonwealth.

On the highly controversial topic of war against non-Catholics, the pronouncements of the late Iberian scholastics were for the most part remarkably consistent applications of their theoretical framework. As on other matters, attitudes towards Moslems and (in some regards even more so) Protestants were harsher than towards the pagan American natives, but it was generally upheld that differences of religion could not constitute just cause for war.[89] In context of the teachings of the Salamanca School, the power ambitions of rulers or the desire to expand the empire were also regarded as illegitimate causes for war. Even idolatry and unnatural sins were not generally regarded by the late Iberian scholastics as sufficient cause for war unless the situation was such that the rights of the innocent were being gravely violated (through practices such as human sacrifice) or that idolaters used violence to oppose the preaching of Christian faith (in which case there was just cause for a defensive war). If non-Christian rulers engaged in human sacrifice, persecution of converted citizens or violent action against missionaries, war might be justified to stop these crimes but this was justified more in terms of the protection of the innocent than on purely religious grounds.[90]

In addition to just cause, the legitimacy of war depended on there being no peaceful alternative course of action reasonably available to solve the dispute. This meant that whenever possible, voluntary arbitration by a third party should be tried in order to avoid war.[91] Given the calamitous material and human costs of war, it is also necessary to ponder whether there are material conditions for victory and to weight the chances of military success against its costs and also the potential losses arising in case of defeat (particularly in offensive wars). Additionally, if there is just cause and war is not avoidable, it must be declared and waged by a legitimate sovereign authority.[92]

The criteria for Just War do not, however, stop at the moment of declaration. A Just War must also be waged justly to remain legitimate.[93] While in principle in a Just War actions are justified by the need to secure victory, the late Iberian scholastics generally agreed that even during wartime it continued to be impermissible to deliberately kill the innocent.[94] It was recognized that the death of innocent people might be unavoidable but it was only admissible if it came about as an accidental effect of an action essential to secure victory and every reasonable effort was made to avoid endangering the lives of peaceful non-combatants. Thus Vitoria (1991, pp. 315–316) provides the example of the bombarding a 'fortress of a city where one knows there are many innocent people, but where it is impossible to fire artillery and other projectiles or set fire to buildings' without harming the innocent and affirms that this is legitimate provided the action is essential to pursue victory in a Just War and that care is taken to minimize the evil effects of the war. Moderation and proportionality are also required in case of victory when it comes to both extracting reparations and imposing punishment.[95] Both should be reasonable and proportional to the wrongs inflicted by the guilty.

Interestingly, Vitoria (1991, p. 307) explicitly recognizes a right (and a duty) of individuals who firmly believe in conscience that a war is unjust to refuse to take part in it: 'if the war seems patently unjust to the subject, he must not fight, even if he is ordered to do so by the prince.'

On the whole, one might regard the positions of the late Iberian scholastics on war as aiming to avoid both what they perceived as the pragmatist and amoral approach that came to be associated with Machiavelli and his disciples and also what they regarded as the naive and dangerous pacifism associated with authors such as Erasmus.[96] But perhaps the best summary of the positions of the Salamanca School on war is offered by Francisco de Vitoria (1991, pp. 326–327) himself, in his notable concluding statements to his lecture on the law of war (*De iure belli*):

> From all this we may deduce a few rules and canons of warfare:
>
> 1. First canon: since princes have the authority to wage war, *they should strive above all to avoid all provocations and causes of war.* . . . It is a mark of utter monstrousness to seek out and rejoice in causes which lead to nothing but death and persecution of our fellow-men, whom God created, for whom Christ suffered death. The prince should only accede to the necessity of war when he is dragged reluctantly but inevitably into it.
> 2. Second canon: once war has been declared for just causes, the prince should press his campaign not for the destruction of his opponents, but *for the pursuit of the justice for which he fights and the defence of his homeland*, so that by fighting he may eventually establish peace and security.
> 3. Third canon: one the war has been fought and victory won, he must use his victory with moderation and Christian

humility. . . . He must give satisfaction to the injured, but as far as possible without causing the utter ruination of the guilty commonwealth.

For Vitoria – as was the case generally for the late Iberian scholastics – every reasonable effort should be made in order to avoid war, given the huge and terrible human costs it involved. Nevertheless, pacifism was regarded as an unrealistic and even irresponsible option. In some circumstances, there were just causes that made war legitimate. In those instances, war itself should be fought – as much as possible – within moral boundaries and humility and moderation was recommended to victors, so that peace and security might be fostered in its aftermath.

## The Ethical and Juridical Framework of the Market

The analysis of the Salamanca School's views on economic matters pursued here shows their consistency within the overall framework of the political, legal and ethical thought of late Iberian scholastics; integration between ethics and economics lies at the heart of the approach employed by the late Iberian scholastics.[97]

As emphasized by Melé (1999, p. 179), this approach is characterized, among other factors, by a realistic natural-law outlook (that takes into account actual human ends without forfeiting an ethical evaluation of those ends) and also by a 'first-person' ethics, in which individual agents – and not society as a whole – are taken to be, at the end of the line, the ones who bear responsibility for formulating moral judgements and deciding in conscience how to act on the market.

### Private property and trade

If one bears in mind the way the late Iberian scholastics attempted to jointly articulate the promotion of the common good with the respect for individual rights, it should not come as a surprise that private property was not regarded by them as an absolute right.[98] It would however be deeply mistaken to infer from this that the School of Salamanca disregarded the importance of private property. On the subject of private property, the late Iberian scholastics started from the traditional Christian assumption the prime goal of the material goods created by God is to allow the flourishing of human life and then followed (and significantly developed) the Thomist line of associating the justification for private property with its importance for the promotion of the common good. As synthesized by Chafuen (2003, p. 33):

> In addition to scriptural references, the Medieval Schoolmen employed logic and reasoning in their defence of private ownership. They posited the convenience of private property for the development. The doctors offered utilitarian arguments to show that goods that are privately owned are better used than are commonly owned goods. This explanation offers a budding theory of economic development: The division of goods and their ultimate possession by private individuals facilitates increased production, and increased production often contributed to the common good.[99]

This is an approach that has traditionally faced difficulties because other aspects of Catholic doctrine downplay the importance of material goods and praise poverty. It is worth pointing out here that while Thomists did traditionally praise voluntary poverty they did not regard it as mandatory. More importantly, they recognized that, in the current situation of mankind (after the Fall), man must generally make use of material goods to pursue many of his goals and so he must be permitted to produce and obtain them through legitimate means.[100]

The Thomist line of reasoning – incorporating earlier insights from Aristotle – consisted in stating that private property did not contradict natural law and that, given man's nature and the demands of life in society, it might be said to be in conformity with the general principles of natural law. In this framework, it was generally recognized that private property brings about individual incentives to work and also has the potential to favour social peace and a better overall use of resources thereby helping promote the common good. Additionally, the conformity of private property with natural law had clear implications for the state. Since property was regarded as rooted in the *ius gentium* it was exclusively dependent on the recognition of the state whose legitimate scope of action was in fact limited by the existence of property rights.[101]

Among the late Iberian scholastics, Domingo de Soto is a good example of the development of the general approach explained above, as he is clear in including private property in the *ius gentium* and deriving property rights from the general principles of natural law. In the process of doing so, he also shows a definite understanding of the 'tragedy of commons' and advances it as one of the central justifications for the existence of private property:

> For the law of nations includes all that men have logically deduced from natural principles. This is clearly shown by examples. Let's remember the natural principle that human life should be maintained and supported in peace and tranquillity. Considering also the premiss that in a corrupted [i.e. fallen] state of nature, if men lived in common they would not live in peace, nor would the fields be fruitfully cultivated, men have deduced that it is more convenient to divide property.[102]

Since the virtues of liberality, hospitality, helping the poor and (reciprocally) gratitude would be impossible if property was held in common, Soto goes as far as assuring that denying private property constitutes heresy.[103]

In the context of the same discussion, Soto answers the common objection that private property is responsible for many fights and conflicts by invoking the distinction between the demands of a small closed group and the complexity of a large open society such as a nation:

> ... the small number of ecclesiastics who take refuge in the cloisters of monasteries is able to live peacefully in community [i.e. with no private property], but that is not possible for the great human nations. What the poet has said, that these words: mine and yours, lead to many disputes and fights, we sincerely recognize; but there would be many more [disputes and fights] if the things were possessed in common.

An additional related reason for property was the conjunction of human self-interest with the scarcity of human goods. In these conditions, private property should be regarded as essential for the proper administration of material goods. Tomás de Mercado provides an eloquent example of this argument:

> We cannot find a person who does not favor his own interests or who does not prefer to furnish his home rather than that of the republic. We can see that privately owned property flourishes, while city- and council-owned property suffers from inadequate care and worse management. . . . It is not easy to explain how important it is for man to know he is the owner of the thing he produces. On the other hand, people treat common enterprises with great indifference. . . . After man's loss of innocence it becomes necessary for each individual to share in the things of this world, in real estate or moveable reaches. . . . If universal love will not induce people to take care of things, private interest will. Hence, privately owned goods will multiply. Had they remained in common possession, the opposite would be true.[104]

The arguments employed by the late Iberian scholastics to defend private property are specially interesting because they manage to incorporate anthropological realism and sound economic principles in a particularly demanding moral framework.[105]

These arguments may (roughly) be grouped in five categories: the existence of private property fosters (although in no way guarantees) a just social order; is necessary for social peace; is appropriate in conditions of scarcity; provides incentives for a better administration of material goods; and facilitates trade and social cooperation.[106]

In what concerns the importance of social cooperation in a complex economy, Mariana shows a clear understanding of the crucial importance of the division of labour and its enormous potential to satisfy human needs:

> Thus He, who gave food and covering to the other animals and armed them against external force by giving some of them horns or teeth or claws, and others swift feet to fly from danger, cast man out among the difficulties of this life, alone, naked and defenceless, as if he had lost his all in a shipwreck. . . . The rest of life is like its beginning, and proves to lack many things which neither an individual nor a small group could obtain for themselves. How much work and industry is involved in combing, spinning and weaving linen, wool and silk. . . . The life of no single man is long enough to obtain all these things, however long he lives, unless the wonder and observation of many men, and collective experience, should come to the rescue.[107]

While the late Iberian scholastics for the most part regarded commercial activities as morally neutral, they showed in some cases a clear understanding of the socially beneficial consequences of trade.[108] Attitudes towards international trade echoed to some extent those on domestic trade but, as already noted earlier, other considerations (particularly on national sovereignty and security) led some authors to have somewhat more restrictive views.[109]

Before concluding this brief overview of the positions of the Salamanca School on private property and trade, reference should be made to the topic of extreme need and its implications.[110]

The Thomist tradition had emphasized that in cases of urgent and manifest necessity, one could make use of property that did not belong to him in order to attend to this situation of extreme need. Cases of extreme need were usually circumscribed to circumstances where there was a clear and imminent danger to the preservation of human life or liberty, although situations of grave need that would evidently lead to extreme need were sometimes deemed as sufficient justification. In this regard, the late Iberian scholastics were no exception, although there were some particularities in their treatment of this subject. First, it was generally made clear that the obligation of the rich to provide for the needs of the poor was founded on charity, not on justice. Second, and to some extent diverging from Aquinas, even when extreme need was regarded as justifying the use of another's property, an obligation to restitute the goods taken was often affirmed. Martín de Azpilcueta provides one of the strongest examples of this position:

> No one is obliged to donate anything to him who is in extreme need: because it suffices that he lends him what is necessary to liberate him from it, and the person in need has no right to take more of the neighbor's estate than its owner, and it is enough, if there is need, that he takes it as a loan and not as his own.[111]

In other words, extreme need could make legitimate the use of goods that belonged to someone else (and imposed on the owner an obligation to lend them to the person in extreme need) but this did not mean that property rights were transferred by that act. As soon as possible, the goods taken as a 'loan' should be devolved to its rightful owner.

While the difficult topic of extreme need may at first sight seem to weaken the scholastics' position, it was nevertheless consistent with their general framework for defending private property. Given that in this framework property is justified because of its numerous and significant benefits for human life and the common good, it logically follows that in those extreme cases where that relationship clearly does not hold, it is human life and the common good that take priority.

**Just price and the subjective theory of value**

The concept of *just price* is probably second only to the condemnation of usury as a source of derision of scholastic economics. As noted by Roover (1958, p. 418):

> In the view of many economists the just price is a nebulous concept invented by pious monks who knew nothing of business or economics and were blissfully unaware of market mechanisms. It is true that certain writers, Catholics and non-Catholics alike, have done their best to accredit this fairy tale and to propagate the notion that the just price, instead of being set by the allegedly blind and unconscionable forces of the market, was determined by criteria of fairness without regard to the elements of supply and demand or at least with the purpose of eliminating the evils of unrestrained competition.

This is however an unfortunate misconception, since it not only distorts the scholastics' views (and particularly those of the Salamanca School), but it also makes it difficult to recognize the important contributions they provided to the theory of value and prices.[112]

As early as the sixteenth century, the prevailing conceptions within scholastic economics already equated to a significant degree the *just price* with the idea of *common estimation*, a notion that was associated with current market valuation taking into account all relevant local circumstances.[113] The most prominent line of dissent from the association of just price with the market price was that of followers of John Duns Scotus, who argued that the just price should be calculated by adding normal profit and risk premiums to costs. Since the late Iberian scholastics provided great contributions to the consolidation and development of the association of the just price with the idea of common estimation (with this in turn depending on local conditions of supply and demand), it is no coincidence that they were generally very critical of the views of Scotus and his followers.

The Salamanca School also provided notable statements anticipating the subjective theory of value. Thus Covarrubias explains that it is human subjective preferences that ultimately determine the value of goods, even if these preferences are 'foolish':

> The value of an article does not depend on its essential nature but on the estimation of men, even if that estimation be foolish. Thus, in the Indies wheat is dearer than in Spain because men esteem it more highly, though the nature of the wheat is the same in both places.[114]

Similarly, Molina distinguishes between the legal price and the natural price by appealing in direct and explicit terms to the principles of the subjective theory of value:

> Another price is that which things have by themselves, independently of any human law or public decree. Aristotle and many others call this the natural price. They call him so not because it doesn't depend to a large extent upon the esteem with which men appreciate some things more than others, as happens with certain precious objects, that sometimes are valued in more than twenty thousand gold coins and more than many other things, which, by their nature are much better and more useful; nor do they call him so because that price doesn't fluctuate and change, since it is evident that it does change; but they call him natural because it is born out of these same things, independently of any human law or public decree, but dependent on many circumstances which make it vary and on the affection and esteem that men have for things according to the several uses in which they can be employed.[115]

It must however be noted that in the late Iberian scholastics also generally included in the notion of just price a legal price legitimately fixed by public authorities. In other words, the notion of *just price* included both the *natural price* (which was necessarily derived from common estimation and thus may be regarded as a market price in the absence of fraud, force, monopoly or monopsony) and the *legal price*.[116] The legal price should be set by a legitimate authority and be in line with the persecution of the common good.

The concern with the common good led some of the late Iberian scholastics to be highly sceptical of legal prices and, in some cases, taking the position of opposing all forms of price regulation. Molina and (even more so) Mariana were critical of price controls that distorted economic conditions and criticized their harmful effects.[117] Azpilcueta explicitly condemned all political controls on prices arguing they were irrelevant in times of abundance and either unworkable or detrimental to the common good in times of scarcity.[118]

**Usury and interest**

The traditional scholastic position on usury was one of clear and unequivocal condemnation, with the term originally encompassing any situation of charging interest on a money loan. This is a topic that requires some precaution as discussions on the treatment of usury in scholastic thought are often superficial and fail to convey how the subject was really treated. As noted by Gregg (2008, p. 74):

> The history of the usury debates is complex and particularly subject to caricature. For our purposes, it suffices to note that while neither Judaism nor Christianity objected to people making honest profits, a question hovered over the matter of whether an honest profit could be earned by selling money: that is, charging a price for money or what we call 'interest'. The early fathers of the Christian Church condemned the charging of interest on a money loan. It was unjust, they maintained, when the borrower was a poor person seeking ways

to survive, while the lender was a wealthy person who had resources to help the poor man if he chose to do so.

The condemnation of charging interest on money loans was based on the traditional reasons that Aquinas had also exposed, namely: that money is sterile (on the sense it was regarded as non-productive by itself); that charging a price (interest) for the use of a perishable (and, bear in mind, sterile) good like money was charging for the same thing twice; and that time could not be sold because it did not belong to any man in particular.[119]

This meant that, initially and as a general principle, all charging of interest (not just some conception excessive interest) on a money loan was to be regarded as illegitimate. Unsurprisingly, throughout the Middle Ages, this led to a wide range of complex and opaque financial contracts constructed in order to evade charges of usury while at the same time allowing lenders to charge interest.[120]

However, while the loan could not intrinsically give rise to the payment of any interest, Aquinas admitted the possibility that the lender might charge payments based on extrinsic reasons associated with the loan. These included losses suffered as a consequence of making the loan (but, for Aquinas, did not include estimated future profits because these are not certain) and, in the case of loans to 'merchants and craftsman' also shared profits from the activities of the enterprise being financed.[121] As noted by Gregg (2008, p. 76), this meant 'an implicit recognition that money is not always sterile' and that at least in some circumstances loaning money as capital might legitimately justify the payment of compensation.

In his analysis of the foreign exchange market, the influential Cajetan (2007) paved the way for widening the exchange transactions deemed legitimate and he also contributed to expand the scope of acceptable payments of compensation in investment contracts, thereby in practice facilitating the practice of business loans.[122]

Generally, the late scholastics – in line with the Roman law tradition – accepted that the payment of compensation on loans could be justified by the titles of *lucrum cessans* (gains that could have been obtained if the money had been invested elsewhere), *damnum emergens* (losses suffered because of the loan), and *poena conventionalis* (penalization for delayed repayment of the loan).[123]

The justification of *lucrum cessans* was generally circumscribed to business loans and so was not equivalent to erasing the condemnation of interest on all loans, but the net effect of all the variations of extrinsic titles allowed was that, in practice, more and more forms of loans (and ways of defending what was in effect the payment of compensation for those loans) were deemed legitimate or could at least be tolerated.

Expressing to a significant degree the changing interpretations of the time, at the Fifth Lateran Council (1512–1517) usury was defined as a profit resulting from the use of something sterile and obtained without labour, cost or risk for the lender. In doing so, Pope Leo X was in effect approving of a wide understanding of extrinsic titles which could be used to justify the payment of compensation for loans. Furthermore, even though condemnation of usury was maintained, it was implicitly acknowledged that 'sterile' money could be made productive if any of the three factors mentioned above was involved in the transaction.[124]

Although they stood firm in their moral condemnation of usury, several of the late Iberian scholastics applied both the possibility of expressing 'gratitude' in monetary terms and the accepted extrinsic titles in ways that legitimized the payment of compensation for money loans to be legitimate in a wide range of situations, particularly (although not exclusively) those related with business transactions.[125]

The outcome of this evolution was largely, as expressed by Roover (1955, p. 173), that 'the lawfulness of interest became a question of formality, that is, of drafting contracts in the proper form'. While this exposed the Church and the scholastics to accusations of hypocrisy, the fact is that by the early sixteenth century there was ample provision in mainstream Catholic doctrine for allowing the payment of compensation for money loans in a wide range of settings.[126]

The analysis above should not however be interpreted as implying that the late Iberian scholastics provided satisfactory answers to all questions regarding the payment of interest. As noted by Rothbard (2006, p. 128), partly because of all their nuances and complexity, the late scholastics' positions on usury were prone (justly or unjustly) to being attacked from both sides: some Protestants (as well as Catholics who sympathized with the Protestant urge to go back to an alleged earlier doctrinal 'purity') could (and did) attack them for weakening the ban on usury while secularists could (and did) attack them for hypocritically keeping the formal prohibition while in practice devising numerous exceptions.

Given the complexity and formalism of their teachings on interest, as well as the apparent contradictions between the proclaimed general moral principles and the accepted business practices, it seems reasonable to agree with Roover (1955, p. 173) and Chafuen (2003, p. 123) when they identify the doctrine of usury as the weakest link in scholastic economics.

**Theories of banking**

In the context of the unprecedented influx of precious metals into the Iberian Peninsula – which transformed cities like Seville into major international financial centres of the time – important questions were also raised about the development of banking and the financing of government expenditure. Pressed by his foreign policy, Charles V frequently resorted to the banking system to fund public spending. This led to the strengthening of bonds between the state and political influential bankers and meant that the insolvency issues of the royal treasury were transmitted to the economy through their implications in the banking system.[127]

The collaboration Huerta de Soto (2006, pp. 79–83) describes is one where bankers were allowed to operate on a fractional-reserve system while the emperor financed his activities through the banking system (including by requesting compulsory loans). In this context, it is not surprising that artificial booms were generated and that financial crisis and bank failures occurred.

The positions of the Salamanca School in what concerns banking can be roughly divided into two main groups. Some of the late Iberian scholastics, including Domingo de Soto and Luis de Molina, were inclined to accept fractional reserve banking – the widespread practice of maintaining only a fraction of demand deposits in liquid reserves and using the remainder to provide loans, with which to pay interest on deposits – as legitimate.[128] Others, such as Saravia de la Calle and Martín de Azpilcueta denounced fractional-reserve practices and stood for full reserve requirements in banking.

The first group justified the acceptability of fractional-reserve banking on the grounds that the bank deposit contract might be regarded as a form of loan to the bank by the depositor (even tough the bank assumes the obligation of repaying the deposit on demand).[129] It should however be noted, that although Molina regarded fractional reserves and the ensuing credit creation as legitimate, he nevertheless warned that this banking practice imposed particular obligations of prudent behaviour on the part of bankers:

> It is important to warn that [bankers] commit mortal sin if they use in their own business dealings so much of the money they hold on deposit that they are later unable, at the right time, to hand over the quantities the depositors request or order to be paid against their deposited funds. . . . In addition, they commit mortal sin if they become involved in business dealings entailing a risk of not being able to return deposits. For example, if they send so much merchandise overseas that, should the ship sink or be captured by pirates, they would not be able to repay deposits even after selling all of their assets. And they are not guilty of mortal sin only when the deal turns out poorly, but also when it turns out well. This is due to the

chance they take of hurting depositors and the guarantors they themselves supply for the deposits.[130]

Members of the second group held quite distinct views on the subject.[131] They criticize bankers for loaning out funds that are in fact demand deposits and stand for a full reserve system, in which banks would get a fee for the safekeeping of deposits but would be unable to engage in credit creation and monetary expansion. Thus Martín de Azpilcueta (2007, pp. 59–60) regards demand deposits as implying that the bank acts as a:

> ... safekeeper, depositary, and guarantor of the money that is given to him or exchanged for something needed by those who give it or send it. This makes him pay the merchants or the people that the depositers choose in a particular way, and, because of this, it is licit that take a just salary from the republic or from the depositing parties. Because this profession and work is useful to the republic and does not possess any iniquity whatsoever, it is just that someone who works earn his wage.

This exchanger's occupation is to receive the money from the merchants; to deposit it; to have it ready; and also to write, keep the books, give an account of the money to everyone with great difficulty, and to run the risk of making a mistake with the accounts and other things. The same thing could be carried out with a contract by which one of the parties commits himself to some people to receive and keep money under deposit, giving, paying, and keeping the books with the people according to the way they tell him to because this is the kind of contract where the activity and work of one is rented out to someone else. Such a contract is specifically provided for by the law and is just and holy.

The two positions – supports for fractional-reserve banking and the alternative system of requiring full reserves on demand deposits – were thus represented within the Salamanca School, in some aspects anticipating theoretical debates that came to take place centuries later.

## Monetary theory and inflation

Cajetan had already taken the first steps in the direction of applying a general theory of value to money but it were the late Iberian scholastics that provided the most decisive and clear contributions on monetary theory and the analysis of inflation.[132] The late Iberian scholastics were particularly concerned with the continued, generalized and sustained rise of prices and eventually came to establish a connection between price inflation and the increase in the money supply that was being primarily fuelled by the imports of precious metals from America.

The first comprehensive treatise on money written by a late Iberian scholastic was the 1550 *Veterum collatio numismatum*, by Diego de Covarrubias y Leyva, which compiled and presented a vast array of historical price statistics and examined the devaluation of Castilian currency.[133] The major theoretical breakthroughs in monetary theory can, however, be attributed to Martín Azpilcueta, the famed *Doctor Navarrus*, of whom Covarrubias was a student. Grice-Hutchinson (1978, p. 104) credits Martín de Azpilcueta as having authored the 'first clear and definite statement of the quantity theory of money that is known to us' and it is in fact hard not be struck by his clarity and consistency considering he was writing in mid-sixteenth century:[134]

> . . . all merchandise becomes more expensive when there is a great need and small quantity of it. Money, inasmuch as it is a thing that may be sold, bartered, or commuted by means of another contract, is merchandise for what we said above and may also become more expensive when there is great need of it and not very much to satisfy this need.
> 
> . . . the rest being the same, in those countries where there is a great lack of money, less money is given for marketable goods, and even for the hands and work of men than where there is an abundance of it. This we can see from experience in France where there is less money than in Spain. Bread, wine, wool, hands, and work cost less. Even in Spain, when there was less money, much less was given for saleable goods, and the hands and work of men, than later when the discoveries of

the Indies covered it in silver and gold. The cause for this is that money is worth more where and when there is a lack of it than where and when there is an abundance.

Azpilcuetas' precise understanding of the core principles of the quantity theory of money was not an isolated case within the late Iberian scholastics. Other authors were also able to extend the application of their sophisticated theory of value to the analysis of money. A few decades later, Molina (2007, pp. 197–198) provided an equally acute understanding of the subject:

> In equal circumstances, the more abundant money is in one place so much less is its value to buy things with, or to acquire things that are not money. Just as the abundance of merchandise reduces their price when the amount of money and quantity of merchants remains invariable, so too the abundance of money makes prices rise when the amount of merchandise and number of merchants remain invariable, to the point where the same money loses purchasing power. So we see that, in the present day, money is worth in the Spanish territories much less than what it was worth eighty years ago, due to the abundance of it. What was bought before for two today is bought for five, or for six, or maybe for more. In the same proportion has the price of salaries risen, as well as dowries and the value of real estate, revenues, benefices, and all other things. . . . Neither is it worth the same in all parts because of this reason, yet it varies according to its abundance and all other circumstances. And this value does not remain unaltered as if it were indivisible, yet fluctuates within the limits defined by the people's estimation, the same as happens with merchandise not appraised by law.

In order to better contextualize the intellectual achievements of the late Iberian scholastics in this domain, one should bear in mind that their contribution came more than 300 years before comparable advances in economic theory were established in the nineteenth- and even twentieth centuries. The ability of the Salamanca School to integrate their analysis of the determination of the value of money in a supply and demand framework in effect represented a unified and general theory of value. This was an achievement that would not be consistently replicated by later economists until the marginalist revolution that took place in the 1870s.[135]

Armed with consistent theories of banking and money the late Iberian scholastics were well equipped to analyse – and more importantly condemn – the inflationary government policies that plagued Spain and eventually played a major role in its ultimate decline as the foremost world power.

As noted above when discussing the Salamanca School's theories of banking, the financial necessities of the Spanish government during this period were immense. The expansion of empire carried with it great demand for government expenditure both internally and abroad and this meant that public debt was a constant burden. In addition to direct interference in the banking system, another method to finance government expenditure was currency debasement. Copper coins in particular – the *véllon* – were subject to successive operations of devaluation and the price inflation that ensued was one of the factors leading to the ultimate triumph of protectionist and mercantilist policies against the generally free trade-oriented policy prescriptions of the Salamanca School.

The prevailing opinion within the Salamanca School was that while it was up to public authorities to determine the standard (monetary) unit of account, the state also had an obligation to ensure that his monetary unit, once established, was permanent.[136] Thus, Tomás de Mercado stated:

> It is universal and necessary for (money) to be any fixed measurement, that is sure and permanent. Everything else can, and even must change, but the measurement must be permanent, because as a fixed sign we can measure the changes of other things.[137]

And, in a similar vein, Mariana (2007, p. 265):

> Weights, measures, and money are, of course, the foundations of commerce upon which rests the entire structure of trade. Most things are sold by weight and measure – but everything is sold by money. Everyone wants the foundations of buildings to remain firm and secure, and the same holds true for weights, measures, and money. They cannot be changed without danger and harm to commerce.
>
> The ancients understood this. One of their major concerns was to preserve a specimen of all these things in their holy temples so that no one might rashly falsify them.

Changes to the monetary unit by the public authorities were considered permissible in times of great crisis but there was widespread condemnation of inflationist policies that led to continual devaluation of money.[138] Equally significant was that Juan de Mariana – the foremost critic of inflationist policies among the late Iberian scholastics – argued that even when currency debasement was admissible it generated an obligation on the part of the king to compensate his subjects once the crisis was over, thereby recognizing that this was in fact a (particularly aggressive) form of taxation. Debasement of money has the effect of reducing the value of the money holdings of citizens to generate resources for public spending and can thus be considered a *de facto* tax.[139]

Mariana (2007, p. 284) in fact went even further and explicitly equated currency debasement by public authorities with theft:

> The king is not free to seize his subjects' goods and thus strip them from their lawful owners. May a prince break into granaries and take half of the grain stored there, and then compensate for the damage by authorizing the owners to sell the remainder at the same price as the original whole? No one would be so perverse as to condone such an act, but such was the case with the old copper coin.

And Mariana also had a crystal clear perception of why such practices were systematically enacted with money but not in other domains of the economy:

> Such things, of course, do not take place in other forms of commerce. They do, however, happen in the arena of money because the king has more power over money than over other things.

Mariana provided numerous examples of the evil effects of past inflationary policies in territories such as Spain, Portugal and England. Referring to monetary policy during the reigns of Henry VIII and Edward VI, Mariana (2007, p. 287) states:

> ... someone who had 400 coins in that money quickly found them reduced to no more than 100. And the cheating continued. When the problems connected with this money did not slacken, a new decree had all that money remitted to the mints in the hope of compensation. Such compensation was never made. An infamous highway robbery! A most disgraceful peculation!

Juan de Mariana did not limit himself to describing and denouncing inflation, he also had a clear understanding – built both on theory and on empirical knowledge of Iberian history and past crisis generated by inflationist policies – that 'currency debasement threatened the entire economic order of the kingdom.'[140] Thus, the special value of Mariana's contributions in this domain lies in the fact that he combined his solid insights on monetary theory with a clear view of the economic, social and political consequences of inflation and the personal courage to publicly explain and denounce them in the strongest terms.[141]

**Taxation and public finance**

As in other pressing matters of the time, the contributions of the late Iberian scholastics in matters of taxation and public expenditure were also influenced by their analysis of current events. The vast economic costs of maintaining a world empire and the perception of domestic waste when it came to public spending led several of the late scholastics to focus on the shortcomings of the state in economic matters.[142]

Given the views of the Salamanca School on political authority and the common good, it should not come as a surprise that they regarded taxation as an acceptable means that legitimate governments might use to finance their necessary expenses, provided the cause for the expenses was indeed just. At the same time, considering the acute political and economic insights into the nature and operation of government developed by the late Iberian scholastics, it is also not surprising that they advised moderation on public expenditure and issued numerous warnings about the many dangers of reckless management of a country's finances and the accumulation of public debt.[143]

The analysis of Domingo de Soto combines all the elements mentioned above. Soto states that taxes are just and generate an obligation (in conscience, and not only for fear of punishment) to pay if they are motivated by a proper cause and the state truly needs them to fulfil its role. However, he also warned that:

> . . . rulers who oppress their peoples with taxes and that demand them not for a legitimate cause, but because of hate or in other to hand out benefits and favors, are reprehended not only by philosophers and historians, but also by the sacred books.[144]

Aware that politicians have an innate tendency to increase public expenditure, Soto warns that one of the 'dangers' that threatens heads of state is that of 'demanding taxes in greater quantity than what the state needs'. This should be a constant concern of rulers, so that 'as soon as the need [that gave rise to a particular tax] ceases, the tax may also cease to be demanded.'[145] Soto also argues for proportional taxation ('one should pay as much more as more abundant riches he possesses and more profits he reports') and emphasizes that if public expenditure is not curbed, the citizens will necessarily be oppressed, for 'as the need of the king's expenditures grows from day to day, the people is also molested from day to day with many taxes.'

There was widespread condemnation by the late Iberian scholastics of excessive taxation as unjust and detrimental to the common good and Molina went as far as affirming not only an obligation of restitution on the part of rulers in such cases but also the principle that individuals might even be morally justified in secretly compensating themselves for the losses derived from unjust taxation.[146]

Perhaps the best way to conclude the overview of this topic is to recall Juan de Mariana's advice when, after condemning in the strongest terms the debasement of money a form to pay for public expenditure, he reflects upon alternative ways to finance government. It is telling that Mariana (2007, p. 299) starts his reflection precisely by advising moderation and recommending that public expenditure be reduced:

> First of all, somehow, court expenditures could be lessened, for reasonable and prudent moderation is more splendid and manifests more majesty than unnecessary and unreasonable consumption.

The analysis of the late Iberian scholastics in matters of public finance and taxation is reminiscent of their whole approach to political economy. It combines a realistic anthropological approach with a sophisticated theoretical framework and a scepticism about the workings of government. The result is a myriad of important insights and contributions that were certainly advanced for the epoch and, on some topics, even when judged by contemporary standards.

## Chapter 3

# Reception and Influence of the Work

The reception and influence exerted by the works and ideas of the Salamanca School can be divided into two major areas. The first corresponds to their practical application in the intense disputations and controversies of their time about the colonization of the 'New World' in America. The second has to do with the impact of the ideas of the late Iberian scholastics in the theological political discussions that assailed Europe in their time and as well as their influence on subsequent authors and the development of ideas in the main fields to which they contributed.

## The Salamanca School and the New World

The (European) discovery of America and the subsequent process of colonization fostered a large number of practical applications of the political thought of the Salamanca School in its time. The theoretical contributions and practical influence of the late Iberian scholastics spanned themes as diverse as international law, individual rights and constitutionalism to economic matters and business ethics, but their participation in the controversies over the status of the native inhabitants of the New World is probably the most widely known and discussed topic in contemporary literature, both at a scholarly and at a popular level. What is not always sufficiently emphasized – but will hopefully become clear in the overall context of the present book – is how much the role of the Salamanca School in these controversies is closely linked with the broader framework of political thought developed and popularized by the School.

The most influential figure in these discussions – Father Bartolomé de Las Casas – was trained at the University of Salamanca. Somewhat ironically, although he was undoubtedly heavily influenced by the doctrines of the School he was not himself a scholar, or at least not one that could be considered in the same league as Vitoria, Soto, Covarrubias, Molina or Suárez.[1] Trained as a lawyer, Las Casas was essentially an activist and a polemist but the combination of those personal features with some of the main Salamancan contributions on individual rights and international law proved to be extremely powerful and assured him long-lasting fame, particularly in debates over slavery, serfdom and colonization. That Las Casas' style was more that of a polemist than of a traditional scholar can be amply confirmed by analysing one of his major works: *In Defense of the Indians*.[2] But although Las Casas is undeniably the most famous activist involved in these controversies, in order to understand the origins of the intense polemics about the New World it is necessary to go back to a sermon by another Dominican friar.

### A revolutionary sermon in Hispaniola

In 1511, at the island of Hispaniola (in the Antilles), a Dominican named Antonio de Montesinos delivered a thundering sermon that put into serious question the accepted methods employed by Spaniards to deal with native Americans and eventually ended up shaking the very foundations upon which the mightiest empire of the World was colonizing the recently discovered territories in America. An account of the Montesinos sermon is described by Bartolomé de Las Casas (1971, pp. 80–81) in the following terms:

> Father Fray Antonio de Montesinos ascended the pulpit and took as the text and foundation of his sermon, which he carried written out and signed by the other friars: 'I am the voice

of one crying in the desert.' . . . 'I have ascended here to cause you to know those sins, I who am the voice of Christ in the desert of this island. Therefore it is fitting that you listen to this voice, not with careless attention, but with all your heart and senses. For this voice will be the strangest you ever heard, the harshest and hardest, most fearful and most dangerous you ever thought to hear.'

And, according to Las Casas, Montesinos made every effort to deliver on his promise:

> This voice cried out for some time, with very combative and terrible words, so that it made their flesh tremble, and they seemed already standing before the divine judgement. . . . 'This voice,' he said, 'declares that you are all in mortal sin, and live and die in it, because of the cruelty and tyranny you practice among these innocent peoples. Tell me, by what right or justice do you hold these Indians in such a cruel and horrible servitude? On what authority have you waged such detestable wars against these peoples, who dwelt quietly and peacefully on their own land? . . . And what care do you take that they should be instructed in religion, so that they may know their God and creator, may be baptized, may hear Mass, and may keep Sundays and feast days? Are these not men? Do they not have rational souls? Are you not bound to love them as you love yourselves? Don't you understand this? Don't you feel this? Why are you sleeping in such a profound and lethargic slumber?'

The powerful sermon apparently failed at changing the minds of those in attendance but the strong reactions it generated were decisive for the reconsideration of the entire colonization process. In addition to that, the chain of events that followed the powerful and controversial sermon of Montesinos contributed to foster intense debate and reflection in the Iberian intellectual context of the time about the universal implications of the general principles of natural law and about (what we would now refer to as) universal human rights.

The immediate reaction of the colonists was to protest against the sermon and ask for the intervention of the Governor. Montesinos, however, not only failed to retract his statements but intensified his condemnation of the behaviour of the colonizers. On the following Sunday, when some of those who took offence at the first sermon were expecting a retraction, Montesinos, according to Las Casas (1971, p. 85) stated:

'I will go back over my knowledge from the beginning, and I will prove that my discourse is without falsehood.' That is, 'I will go back to rehearse from the beginning my knowledge and the truths which I preached to you last Sunday, and I will show that those words of mine which embittered you are true.'

News of the dispute quickly reached Spain and in March 1512 both the King and the Superior of the Dominicans in Spain condemned Montesinos' words and demanded that the Dominicans in Hispaniola immediately stopped preaching their disruptive doctrines about the mistreatment of Indians and the violation of their rights by the European colonizers.[3]

In spite of the high level pressures, the Dominican friars did not comply and the issue evolved until eventually both sides (the Dominicans and the colonists) sent special emissaries to make their respective cases heard in court. The Dominican representative sent to Spain was Montesinos himself and his words made such an impression on King Ferdinand that he made arrangements for a group of scholars to study the issue and propose new and more adequate laws. This initiative led to the first set of legislation dealing thoroughly with the treatment of native Americans by the colonizers: the Laws of Burgos, promulgated on December 1512 and amended in 1513.[4] The Laws of Burgos included several provisions for the religious conversion and education of the Amerindians, but also extensive regulation on the treatment and working conditions that the Spanish ought to confer to them. Although the immediate concrete effects of these laws in America were at best moderate, the process spearheaded a long and intense debate that would eventually lead to the more elaborate New Laws of 1542 and to the famous disputation between Bartolomé de Las Casas (who had attended the 1511 Montesinos sermon even though he did not immediately become converted to the cause of defending the of the Indians) and Juan Ginés de Sepúlveda.

Before proceeding to elaborate upon some of the key topics of the controversies, it is worth recalling at this point that both Antonio de Montesinos and Bartolomé de Las Casas had been educated at Salamanca. The education the two Dominicans received there was certainly not neutral in what concerned the positions they would later assume concerning the controversies about the New World. As remarked by Watner (1987, p. 296), there is a good case to be made for the existence of a close linkage between the intellectual climate fostered by the Salamanca School and the discussions that ensued about the colonization of America and the universality of human rights:

> This controversy over the treatment of the Indians, and the eventual formulation of the much celebrated Laws of the Indies in 1542, could never have come about without the theological-juridical and Thomist tradition of the Dominican order. Those first missionaries did not protest solely from the natural and Christian impulse of humanity and compassion; they were learned men formed in Salamanca and other centers of Dominican instruction in Spain.

**The social experiments of Bartolomé de Las Casas**

The one point where there was wide ranging public (internal) consensus was that the ultimate legitimacy of Spanish actions in America rested on executing a mandate for the conversion of Native Americans to Christianity. As noted by Hanke (2002, p. 147):

All theorists whose opinions were sought by the crown in 1512 agreed, however, as had all Spaniards since the Indies were first discovered, that the papal concession and that alone justified sufficiently the Spanish title and that this concession was given for the conversion of the Indians.

There was, however, right from the beginning considerable disagreement both on the proper methods for enacting that conversion and – even more crucially – on the nature and status of those that were to be converted.

A common purpose of all of Las Casas' experiments and of his activism in general was to try to put an end to the oppressive *encomienda* system, which placed pieces of land and groups of Indians under tutelage of European colonizers, which could explore their labour and exact tribute while having the formal obligation of educating them in the ways of Christian faith and civilization. While the Amerindians were not formally slaves, their material condition amounted in fact to a situation of quasi-serfdom, guaranteed by the superior military might of the Spanish and prone to abuses such as the ones vividly described in Montesinos' sermons and on many of Las Casas' writings.[5] Las Casas, and other ecclesiastics who shared his cause, wanted to demonstrate that the *encomienda* was both immoral and unnecessary. Given the solid and very vocal opposition of the Spanish *encomenderos*, the experiments were enacted in order to try to prove that alternative methods of relationship with the Amerindians could be enacted and provide more acceptable results.

The main practical questions concerned the potential of Amerindians to live in communities that resembled those of Christian Europe and the possibility of converting them and so to colonize the New World by peaceful means. Las Casas – after the 'conversion' that led him to become the most prominent defender of the Indians – strongly believed in positive answers to those crucial questions while most of the conquistadors and *encomenderos* strongly believed otherwise.

The intense controversy over these questions paved the way for the remarkable social experiments carried out largely under

Las Casas' guidance in the New World. The combination of the overwhelming power of the Spanish Crown with the intellectual renewal spurred by the late Iberian scholastics provide an environment uniquely open to experimentation that Las Casas explored to the full. The experiments would have been impossible without royal support and the fact that way were carried out strongly suggests that getting the right answers to the questions referred above was deemed very important for the rulers of the time. As summed up by Pagden (2004, p. xxiv):

> Las Casas was always able to play upon a deep moral unease within royal and ecclesiastical circles. The Spanish Crown had a long history of anxiety over the legitimacy of its military ventures and ever since the twelfth century Castillian monarchs had sought the advice of jurists and theologians as to how to conduct, or to seem to conduct, their affairs. They may not have always taken this advice too literally for, as the greatest of the Spanish theologians of the sixteenth century Francisco de Vitoria once observed, kings are necessarily pragmatic beings forced 'to think from hand to mouth'. But the Spanish monarchs, the self-styled champions of Christendom, lived in constant fear of finding themselves out of favour with their God.[6]

The 1513 amendments to the Laws of Burgos had provisions for allowing American Indians judged to be able to live like Christians in politically organized communities to be set free and gave rise to the first type of experiments.[7] These experiments tried to determine whether the American natives could indeed do so by setting up American natives in specially conceived villages mirroring Spanish institutions, under more or less direct supervision by clerics. These experiments were for the most part complete failures, an outcome that on hindsight should not be regarded as surprising given that the Amerindians were removed from their traditional communities and place in what was (to them) a completely strange mode of social organization.

A second type of experiment tried to explore the possibility of peacefully establishing colonies of European farmers instead of resorting to the *encomienda* system.[8] These efforts also ended up in failure, partly because the interests and patterns of behaviour on the ground made it extremely hard to sustain prolonged peaceful relationships between any European colonizers and the American natives and also because it was simply untenable to have large numbers of Europeans moving to America to work as farmers or artisans at the time. Despite the intentions of Las Casas and other ecclesiastics, their efforts were bound to fail for, as pointed out by Hanke (2002, p. 71), it was that, understandably, most 'Spaniards willing to risk their lives and fortunes in the New World were not interested in becoming farmers, even if they had been such in Spain, but man of wealth and position.'

A third type of experiment led by Las Casas – and one that, unlike the others, achieved some degree of success – consisted in trying to convert the Indians to Christianity exclusively through peaceful means. These (at the time) radical experiments in effect mirrored the doctrine pronounced in 1537 by Pope Paul III in his bull *Sublimis Deus*.[9] In the bull, those that held that the 'Indians of the West and the South, and other people of whom we have recent knowledge should be treated as dumb brutes created for our service' were condemned for being at the service of the 'enemy of the human race, who opposes all good deeds in order to bring man to destruction' and the proper position for Catholics was described as follows:

> We . . . consider, however. That the Indians are truly man and that they are not only capable of understanding the catholic faith but, according to our information, they desire exceedingly to receive it. Desiring to provide ample remedy for these evils, we declare . . . that, notwithstanding whatever may have been to the contrary, the said Indians and all other people who may later be discovered by Christians, are by no means to be deprived of their liberty or the possession of their property,

even though they be outside the faith of Jesus Christ; and that they may and should, freely and legitimately, enjoy their liberty and the possession of their property; nor should they be in any way enslaved; should the contrary happen it shall be null and of no effect.

By virtue of our apostolic authority, we declare . . . that the said Indians and other peoples should be converted to the faith of Jesus Christ by preaching the word of God and by example of good and holy living.[10]

These positions were fully in line with (and influenced by) the teachings of the Salamanca School and Las Casas' courageous (although not always realistic) initiatives on the ground were a literal application of those ideas. At the Vera Paz experiment that took place in Guatemala from around 1537 until the 1550s, Las Casas took upon himself and his fellow Dominicans the task of achieving the peaceful and voluntary conversion of the inhabitants of Tuzulutlán, a province which the Spaniards had so far been unable to conquer militarily due to the difficulties of the terrain and the military skills of the natives.[11] Interestingly, the first contact with the chieftain was carried out by merchants who used to trade in the area, and whom Las Casas instructed to sing inspirational verses and to suggest that the community ought to invite the wise Dominicans friars to learn what they had to teach about religion. Remarkably, the chieftain appears to have ultimately acceded to the request and, under Dominican influence, peacefully converted to Christianity, ceasing the worship of pagan idols and forbidding the traditional practices of human sacrifice. The Spanish colonists, however, were not pleased and a long dispute erupted over the following years, with each side (Dominicans and nearby *encomenderos*) claiming the other was lying and sabotaging their best efforts on behalf of the Crown of Spain. After many episodes, these efforts to peacefully convert the Amerindians ultimately collapsed after a major pagan revolt against (both European and native American) Christians broke out in 1555.[12]

Despite all their shortcomings and limited results, the social experiments enacted under the leadership of Las Casas and his fellow Dominicans, nevertheless remain fascinating illustrations of how ideas largely inspired by the Salamanca School were put into practice in the New World.

## Just titles and the disputation between Las Casas and Sepúlveda

In addition to his social experiments, Las Casas' tireless campaigning against the *encomienda* system as it was practised in America was one of the main factors pushing forward legislation such as the New Laws of 1542.[13] The instructions of the Spanish Crown ordered the humane treatment of the Indians, emphasized – in line with the late Iberian scholastics – that they were to be considered free men and not slaves by nature and greatly limited the prospects of the *encomienda* system. The reaction of the European *encomenderos* was fierce and often brutal (even towards royal officials) and, with a strong combination of interests lined up against them, it is not surprising that the strict regulations favoured by Las Casas went largely unenforced in distant America and were ultimately for the most part either revoked or forgotten.

Still, despite the ultimate practical outcome, the political debate that took place between defenders of the rights of the American Indians and defenders of the rights of the *encomenderos* was significant and left permanent marks for the future.

The intellectual and political confrontation over the colonization of the New World reached its symbolic peak in the famous 1550 disputation between Juan Ginés de Sepúlveda and Bartolomé de Las Casas.[14] Following the discontent among the Spanish colonizers over the demands of the New Laws of 1542, Sepúlveda composed a work entitled *Democrates secundus*, in which he argued that it was just to force the Indians into submission by arms if no other way is feasible, because they were slaves by nature. Given the inferior condition of Amerindians, if they refused to peacefully submit to the superior Europeans there was – according to Sepúlveda – a just cause to wage war against them.

This was in direct and frontal opposition to the doctrines defended by the main authors of the Salamanca School, and particularly its founder Francisco de Vitoria.[15] Underlying the perspectives of the late Iberian scholastics was the notion of the universality of the principles of natural law. As noted by Hamilton (1963, p. 19):

> Natural law was assumed to exist among all peoples, not merely among Christians; it was a natural system of ethics which neither depended on nor contradicted Christian revelation but could stand by itself.

On his extended analysis of the legitimacy of Spanish actions in America, Vitoria had started by inquiring whether the American natives had true dominion over their land upon Spanish arrival. On this point, after analysing the main claims disputing the rights of the American Indians, Vitoria (1991, pp. 250–251) was unequivocal:

> The conclusion of all that has been said is that the barbarians undoubtedly possessed as true dominion, both public and private, as any Christians. That is to say, they could not be robbed of their property, either as private citizens or as princes, on the grounds that they were not true masters.

Vitoria then proceeded to refute, one by one, the unjust titles by which the Spanish claimed to legitimately rule the American Indians and also to lay out what just titles might come into effect for them to lawfully come under Spanish rule.[16] Vitoria refuted as unjust titles claims that either the emperor or the pope ought to be considered temporal rulers of the whole world; that possession of the New World might be justified by rights of discovery (untenable for the lands were not unoccupied); that the unbelief or the sins of the pagans justified Spanish rule[17]; that the American Indians had freely chosen to come under Spanish rule; and that a special gift from God had granted Spanish rule over the unbelievers. As just titles, Vitoria (1991, p. 278) recognized, first of all, that 'Spaniards have the right to travel and dwell in those countries, so long as they do no harm to the barbarians, and cannot be prevented by them from doing so.' He also considered that they could legitimately 'preach and announce the Gospel in the land of the barbarians' (p. 284), protect converts, defend the innocent, and come to the aid of allies and friends in a just war. Spanish rule might also be legitimately established if it was the result of a genuinely free and voluntary election by the American Indians. More ambiguously, Vitoria (1991, p. 287) included in the list of just titles, the possibility that, in some circumstances (viz. if most of the population had converted to the Christian faith), 'the pope might have reasonable grounds for removing their infidel masters and giving them a Christian prince'; he also admitted – 'though certainly not asserted with confidence' (p. 290) that the generalized mental incapacity of Indians, if proven, might justify Spanish rule, as long as it aimed at their best interest, and not only at furthering the interests of Spaniards.

Despite some ambiguity and possible inconsistency in some of the just titles asserted by Vitoria, the overall inclination of his position is clear and his condemnation of Spanish methods of colonization is made explicit in his general conclusion (1991, pp. 291–292), where he suggests the trade-based Portuguese model as a preferable alternative mode of interaction with the non-converted:

> . . . the barbarians have a surplus of many things which the Spaniards might exchange for things which they lack. Likewise, they have many possessions which they regard as uninhabited,

which are open to anyone who wishes to occupy. Look at the Portuguese, who carry on a great and profitable trade with similar sorts of peoples without conquering them.

As in other domains, Vitoria set the tone for the positions of the Salamanca School in this subject and this theoretical framework was one of the key reasons why in 1548 Melchor Cano and Bartolomé de Carranza (both of them Dominicans, acquaintances of Las Casas, and theologians at Salamanca) and Diego de Covarrubias recommended that Sepúlveda's *Democrates secundus* be denied the official licence for publication in Spain for its grave doctrinal errors and its offensive tone against the American Indians. Sepúlveda, the official chronicler of Charles V, was both humiliated and enraged by the decision and when the king in 1550 ordered the suspension of all conquests in America to evaluate their legitimacy, he readily agreed to stand against Las Casas in the meeting convened at Valladolid to judge on this ponderous matter.

The specific issue the emperor Charles V wished to be thoroughly discussed was:

> Is it lawful for the King of Spain to wage war on the Indians, before preaching the faith to them, in order to subject them to his rule, so that afterward they may be more easily instructed in the faith?[18]

The eminent panel of judges (among them Domingo de Soto, who was entrusted with the task of synthesizing the arguments of the contending parties) appointed by the powerful Council of the Indies heard from Las Casas and Sepúlveda separately and so no direct personal debate occurred. Nevertheless, the Valladolid sessions made the contrast of arguments quite clear.

Sepúlveda's arguments were essentially fourfold: the American Indians were in a condition of natural slavery due to their primitive development and so it was right and proper to subjugate them by force if necessary; practices of idolatry, cannibalism and human sacrifice were just causes for punitive war; the fact that innocent human beings were routinely sacrificed legitimized intervention in their defence; and propagation of the true faith was also a legitimate cause for war since it facilitates conversion and the work of missionaries.[19] Las Casas' lengthy rebuttals emphasized (repeatedly) several key points: that Sepúlveda provided a greatly distorted picture of Amerindians, since there was ample evidence they were not in fact brutes but quite rational and in some aspects even more developed than the Christians who aimed to rule over them; that the teachings of Christ obliged Christians to use peaceful means of conversion; and that the Spanish Crown had no jurisdictional powers to punish the wrongdoings of the native Americans. More problematically, Las Casas' urge to defend the Indians against Sepúlveda's arguments led him to provide some justification for acts of human sacrifice and cannibalism as being essential to the native's religion and a lesser evil when compared to the consequences of waging war against an entire people.[20]

The judges at Valladolid did not reach a final collective verdict (with both Las Casas and Sepúlveda claiming they had won the disputation) but Las Casas' defence of the rights of Amerindians constitutes a major – if understandably imperfect and incomplete – stepping stone in advancing the cause of universal human rights. In his defence and activism, Las Casas essentially provided a radical application of the teachings of the Salamanca School.

Regardless of the formal outcome of the Valladolid junta, the disputation is symbolic of the two positions being confronted and stands as one of the foremost examples of the time of the application of the doctrines of the Salamanca School on individual rights, Just War and international law. Sepúlveda, a learned and well read scholar, certainly stood for the interests of the *encomenderos* but his confrontation with Las Casas can be taken, to some extent, as representative of a broader intellectual confrontation since, as pointed out by Carro (1971, p. 247), 'if Sepúlveda represented anything else, it was the old European ideology, superseded in Spain by men like Francisco de Vitoria and Domingo de Soto, who taught at Salamanca at the time of Sepúlveda's return to Spain.'

## Assessing the Legacy of Las Casas and the Controversies over the New World

Given the influential and widely publicized nature of Las Casas' activism and his works, it is comprehensible that his figure and legacy continue to generate substantial controversy.[21] It is not possible here to suggest in what way these controversies ought to be settled but it is worth pointing out that Las Casas has had a long history of fierce critics and detractors, starting, of course, with the powerful *encomenderos* of his time.

The traditional line of criticism levied against Las Casas is that, by way of gross statistical errors and grave distortion of facts in his denouncements of the treatment of Amerindians, he helped to create a 'Black Legend' about the Spanish colonization of America.[22] Both the hyperbolic style and the lack of rigour of Las Casas in his factual descriptions make him an easy target for this type of criticism but, whatever the ultimate judgement may be on each particular accusation levied against the Dominican reformer, it is probably wise to keep in mind a point expressed, among others, by Comas (1971, p. 489):

> It is known to all that Fray Bartolomé's combative ardour stressed the dark side of the Conquest in order to prove that the Indians needed aid and protection against their exploitation, unjust treatment, and extermination. No one accepts the figures he employed in his arguments; on the other hand, there is abundant and authoritative testimony to the reality of the things he denounced.

Las Casas can also be charged with having an overly naïve view of the Amerindians and their motivations, sometimes treating them in his writings as a sort of 'noble savages' who apparently could do no wrong and reacted only to Spanish provocations. This was probably one of the root causes of the general failure of the social experiments he set up.

Additionally, Las Casas' initial proposal that Amerindians be replaced by African slaves as workers in America does not bode well for his role as precursor of universal human rights.[23] Even there, however, it is important to note that Las Casas was in this regard fully in tune with the prevailing ideas of the time.[24] At the time, as noted by Bataillon (1971, p. 417), their 'appearance, so different from that of whites and Indians, and the contrast between their physical robustness and mental "simplicity" caused them to be regarded as the very type of peoples who were "naturally slaves," according to Aristotle'. It is also important to stress that later in life Las Casas changed his position after becoming convinced that the slavery of Africans was also unjust.

An alternative line of criticism against Las Casas is that of characterizing him as an agent of 'ecclesiastical and political imperialist domination of Indomerica by Spain'.[25] This revisionist account of Las Casas as an 'imperialist' is based on the Dominican's ultimate objective of converting the Amerindians to Christianity and on the limited beneficial effects his actions had on the lives of American natives.[26]

Not withstanding all the controversies, what can be stated with certitude is that the actions, motivations and ideas of Las Casas (as well as the confrontation with his opponents) must be analysed in the context of intellectual trends that were to a large extent shaped by the Salamanca School. As pointed out by Carro (1971, p. 237):

> Las Casas was in no sense an isolated product of sixteenth-century Spain. As *encomendero* and conquistador, as a *clérigo*, and after his conversion, when he enlisted under the banner of the first Dominican missionaries in the New World on Española, and still later, when he entered the Dominican order as he neared his forty-eighth year, Las Casas was always a man of his

time, with ideological, social, and political roots in European mentality and customs. The same can be said of his adversaries, *encomenderos*, conquistadors, and even some missionaries. All, then, had European roots in a long history when, in 1511, after the celebrated sermon of Father Antonio Montesinos, spokesman for the Dominicans on Española, the controversy over the Indians burst forth.

Regardless of the (symbolical and historical) importance that one attributes to Montesinos and (naturally even more so) to Las Casas, the broader setting of ideas and beliefs that helped frame and define their actions must be kept in mind in order to comprehend them fully. In fact, even though the vivid controversies over the New World will always tend to be the most popular topic concerning the influence of the School of Salamanca, the more lasting influence of the ideas of the late Iberian scholastics certainly came about through their direct and indirect impact on generations of subsequent authors.

## Theological-Political Impact and Influence on Subsequent Authors

Given the late Iberian scholastics' central role in the development of the Catholic theological and political responses to Protestant challenges in the sixteenth and seventeenth centuries, one way of evaluating the reception and impact of the Salamanca School in its time is to look at the outcomes of the Counter-Reformation movement itself. While Protestantism was not eradicated and came to successfully endure in large parts of Europe, the post-Tridentine Roman Church nevertheless was able to weather the Protestant storm relatively well. Partly due to the doctrinal work of the late scholastics and to the internal reforms enacted in the Council of Trent, the initial fears that the whole edifice of the Roman Church might collapse never came close to becoming reality. Additionally, initial losses to Protestants came to be partly reversed, so that by the end of sixteenth century the Counter Reformation and its political allies throughout Europe had managed to recover about one third of those losses.[27]

In this context, it's worth recalling that one of Suárez' major works – his 1613 *Defensio fidei* – was written, building upon Bellarmine's efforts, to refute the claims of James I about the divine right and absolute power of kings. Against these Suárez established a clear distinction between the divine right of papal authority aimed at spiritual ends and the political power of secular authorities, which only indirectly is derived from God and whose concrete forms are only of human – not divine – right.[28] The position of Suárez, which would ultimately be largely superseded by the triumph of absolutist conceptions of the state, was, as noted by Rommen (1945, p. 546), that:

> ... while the Church's end is supernatural, the state's end is a natural one: the good status and the perfect order of the common good in the sphere of secular life. Hence political power is called secular and temporal. Furthermore, whereas the Church is necessarily universal and unique, i.e., catholic, the pluralism of the states is quite natural according to the nature of the secular end. Yet even if the rather utopian dream of a world state could be accepted, this would not change the fact that the end of this *civitas maxima* is still secular and temporal.

Partly due to the Protestant Reformation and also to the rising and increasingly centralized national states, the prevailing trend – both in Protestant and Catholic kingdoms – ultimately leaned more and more towards the unification of spiritual and temporal powers in the figure of the absolute monarch. In this sense, although the late Iberian scholastics provided the main line of theoretical resistance to the rise of the absolute state, their positions did not for the most part prevail.[29]

It is important to note here, as Skinner points out (1978, p. 184), that some aspects of Suárez' theory of sovereign power were picked up by later defenders of absolutism:

> At an intellectual level, the no less important result was the establishment of a vocabulary of concepts and an accompanying pattern of political argument which Grotious, Hobbes, Pufendorf and their successors all adopted and developed in building up the classic version of the natural-law theory of the State in the following century.

But despite the notable influence of the late Iberian scholastics – and particularly Suárez – on these authors they, unlike later defenders of absolutism, were still on traditional Thomist natural law ground, which was incompatible with the divine right of kings and the absolutist conception of the state. Evidence of this is that even later Jesuits – faced with the need to accommodate the political trends of their time – for the most part distanced themselves from Suárez' conception of consent and political power. As pointed out by Höpfl (2004, pp. 261–262):

> ... although Suárez's authority for later Jesuits was enormous, the pactum-motif in his thought did not survive into later Jesuit treatments of the topic. It was insecurely located, and was irredeemably associated with what, in most places, became a thoroughly unrespectable hostility to absolute monarchy.

While there were Protestant currents that emphasized resistance and even popular sovereignty, the net effect of the Reformation was – despite the best efforts of the late Iberian scholastics – one of strengthening the movement towards absolutism.[30]

It would however be a mistake to reduce the discussion of the influence of the late Iberian scholastics to the topic of the trend towards absolutism that prevailed in their time and to the doctrines of Suárez, even though he is the most referenced of the Salamanca authors in contemporary Anglo-Saxon studies of the history of political thought.[31]

The Salamanca School's contributions to just war theory also proved influential for subsequent authors who devoted themselves to the topic. As noted by Reichberg *et al* (2006, pp. 288–290) commenting on the historical significance and subsequent influence of Vitoria's of *De indis* and *De iure belli*:[32]

> Delivered in 1539, and first published in 1557, the two lectures were destined to enjoy great notoriety. From Molina and Suárez onwards, philosophers and jurists would use Vitoria's writings as an essential point of reference for normative thinking about international relations.
> [. . .]
> Written on the eve of the sectarian strife that was soon to engulf Europe, Vitoria's emphasis on natural law would have a formative influence on the development of the modern, post-Westphalian conception of the legitimate use of force by sovereign states, wherein the *ius ad bellum* (the right to go to war) is framed in secular rather than religious reasons.

Closely linked with just war theory were, of course, the Salamanca School's pioneering contributions to the development of (broadly defined) international law.[33] As was already discussed, the period in which the late Iberian scholastics lived posed numerous challenges in terms of international relations. The epoch was particularly suited for systematic reflections on international law and so it is not surprising that the late scholastics became forerunners of Hugo Grotius in this domain.[34]

It is also important to consider that in some cases indirect influences may be equally or more powerful than direct ones. In the case of Grotius, for example, the School of Salamanca exerted its influence not only directly but also through indirect means. Consider Fernando Vázquez de Menchaca, a humanist born in 1512 who obtained his licenciate degree at Salamanca in 1549 and accompanied Philip II to the final session of the Council of Trent.[35] Vázquez – who was a major source for Grotius and whom he considered the 'pride of Spain' – developed a large part of his work as a response to the contributions of Domingo de Soto. Thus, in addition to direct influences by the Thomist late Iberian scholastics, by incorporating and developing Vázquez ideas, Grotius was implicitly working at least partly within a framework whose boundaries had been defined by the contributions of the Salamanca School.

Through direct and indirect means, the influence of the political and economic doctrines of the late Iberian scholastics spread out throughout Europe and other regions of the world which were exposed to European contact.[36] Suárez, Azpilcueta and Molina all taught in Portugal while Portuguese authors such as Pedro de Fonseca (1528–1599) had developed influential contributions in their own right.[37] Among others, Antonino Diana (1585–1663) and Martino Bonacina (1585–1663) developed late scholastic ideas in Italy. The Spanish Jesuit Antonio de Escobar spread them in France (being attacked by Pascal for his laxness in the condemnation of usury) while Leonard Lessius (1554–1623) – a friend of Molina and another important source for Grotius – became highly influential in the Netherlands.[38] In Germany, Pufendorf (1632–1694) also reflected the influence of the Salamanca School, even if he, not infrequently, sought to argue against the ideas of the late Iberian scholastics.

Referring to the (often overlooked) role of the late Iberian scholastics on the development and transmission of a 'Spanish natural law school' that combines principles of Roman Law with Aristotelian and Thomist principles, Gordley (2006, pp. 9–10) states:

> Few people today are familiar even with the names of its leaders: for example, Domingo de Soto (1494–1560), Luis de Molina (1535–1600) and Leonard Lessius (1554–1623), and yet, as I have shown elsewhere, they were the first to give Roman Law a theory and a systematic doctrinal structure. Their work deeply influenced the 17th century founders of the northern natural law school, Hugo Grotius (1583–1645) and Samuel Pufendorf (1632–1694) who disseminated their conclusions through northern Europe, paradoxically, at the

very time that Aristotelian and Thomistic philosophy was falling out of fashion.[39]

Even the works of Hobbes—who was certainly not a defender of scholasticism—reflected to some extent late scholastic political thought. As noted by Burns (2006, p. 132):

> Hobbes' attack on the schoolmen – from whose works, nonetheless, he took more of his ideas than he cared to acknowledge – indicates, again, that the doctrine he had received at the turn of the century was still to the fore some fifty years later.

Locke was a similarly fierce critic of the scholastic method, characterizing the 'schoolmen' as the 'great mint-masters' of empty and obscure terms with 'little or no significance' in his 1690 *Essay Concerning Human Understanding*.[40] Nevertheless, and probably even more so than what happens with Hobbes, it is possible to find some of the core ideas developed by the late Iberian scholastics incorporated in the works of Locke. This association is emphasized by Skinner (1978, p. 174):

> If we glance forward, for example, to John Locke's *Two Treatises of Government*, we find him reiterating a number of the most central assumptions of the Jesuit and Dominican writers. He agrees with their analysis of the *ius naturale*, declaring that reason 'is that law' and that the same law must also be treated as 'the will of God'. He agrees with their sense of the pivotal role which ought to be assigned to the *ius naturale* in any legitimate political society, describing it as 'an eternal rule to all men' and insisting that all the enactments of our legislator must be 'conformable' to its demands. And when he turns to consider how it is possible for a political society based on this law to be brought into existence, he endorses both the main arguments which the Jesuits and Dominicans had already advanced.[41]

Regardless of these and other connections that can be established, it is however undeniable that Locke – like other Protestant authors who to some extent incorporated ideas developed by the Salamanca School – expressed highly unfavourable views about scholasticism. One possible way to reconcile these two aspects is to bear in mind the political and religious conditions of late-seventeenth-century Europe. As suggested by Rothbard (2006, p. 316):

> The deep affinity between Locke and Scholastic thought has been obscured by the undeniable fact that to Locke, Shaftesbury and the Whigs, the real enemy of civil and religious liberty, the great advocate of monarchical absolutism, during the late seventeenth century and into the eighteenth century, was the Catholic Church. . . . For the Reformation, after a century, had succeeded in taking the wraps off monarchical tyranny in the Catholic as well as Protestant countries.

It is also worth mentioning that even though Adam Smith broke with scholastic tradition in several regards, it is possible to identify the linkages through which at least some of the ideas and methods of the late scholastics made an impact on him. Smith's teacher, Francis Hutcheson, was significantly influenced by the thought of the late scholastics and works of both Grotius and Pufendorf were part of Adam Smith's library.[42]

Also in the domain of economic theory, it's worth noting that the Salamanca School's theory of value was likely influential in later developments of the marginal utility theory of value by Abbé Ferdinando Galiani, whose work includes a quotation from Diego de Covarrubias.[43]

A final reference is due to the theoretical influence of the Salamanca School in the American continent, an aspect which is often superseded by the much greater attention devoted to the controversies about the New World that are the focus of the first part of this chapter. As would be expected, the influence of the School of Salamanca naturally extended to the American continent, particularly in the territories where Spanish influence was more significant. A particularly good example of this influence is the School of Salamanca's strong connections with the University of San Marcos, in Lima, Peru. San Marcos – officially founded in 1551 – was created with an organizational model and plans of studies that closely mirrored those of the University of Salamanca, in addition to having in the initial faculty several professors educated at Salamanca.[44] The works of the most prominent authors of the School of Salamanca – such as Francisco Vitoria and Domingo de Soto – were used as textbooks and their Thomist outlook provided the basic framework within which specifically American issues were studied.[45]

Overall it's possible to conclude that the wide range of topics to which the late Iberian scholastics contributed was matched by the diversity of the direct and indirect ways they influenced later authors and schools of thought. While these influences are not always obvious at first sight, a careful study of the genealogy of ideas makes clear the lasting impact of some of their main contributions of the Salamanca School even in areas where their preferred methodological approach was ultimately abandoned.

Chapter 4

# Relevance of the Work Today

The case for the contemporary relevance of the Salamanca School can be made from several different perspectives. The need to comprehend the history of ideas and the specific insights provided by the late Iberian scholastics and their methods both constitute reasons for the continued relevance of their work. This chapter analyses this relevance first in the domains of political philosophy, law and history; secondly, in terms of political economy; thirdly, on Catholic social thought; and finally in international affairs and war.

## Political Philosophy, Law and History

The most obvious and direct way in which the work of the Salamanca School is relevant for contemporary political philosophy and law is through the particular blend of Aristotelianism and Thomism it offers. Standing at a time of intense change in politics as well as religion, the late Iberian scholastics attempted to develop a natural-law approach that remained faithful to the traditional Christian conception of the common good while at the same time paving the way for the recognition of a significant domain for individual rights. While shying away from relativist positions, the Salamanca School nevertheless provides a conception of human nature and political organization that is generally much more fitted than its predecessors (and many of its successors as well) to accommodate diversity and (at least some types of) pluralism on solid foundations.

While separating conceptually the domains of theology and philosophy, the specific approach of the Salamanca School to political philosophy and law has, of course, important links with its theology and metaphysics.[1] In fact, another of its most relevant features in contemporary settings is the path it suggests to conciliate faith and reason. In this regard, while Molina's metaphysics are arguably the most sophisticated and interesting of all the late Iberian scholastics, they have been somewhat less influential than Suárez's.[2] Perhaps due to Suárez greater accessibility or to his suggestive rearrangement of Thomist elements, he has notably influenced, both directly and indirectly, authors as diverse as Christian Woff (1679–1754), Gian Battista Vico (1688–1744), Arthur Schopenhauer (1788–1860) and Martin Heidegger (1889–1976).[3] The contemporary relevance of Suárez can similarly be ascertained by the realization that in several important ways, he actually 'anticipates much of the thinking about essence, existence and identity of late twentieth-century analytical metaphysics' (Haldane, 2004, p. 6).

The contemporary relevance of the late Iberian scholastics should not, however, be circumscribed to the domain of the metaphysical foundations of politics or to the conciliation of faith and reason, for their ideas about the role of reason in a natural law framework are similarly important. Against the positions of sceptics about the faculties of human reasoning, the authors of the Salamanca School resorted and solidified the Thomist stance that human reason has the ability to understand the general principles of natural law and thus that political society can be structured on rational grounds.[4] In this regard, among recent conservative and libertarian scholars their approach to political thought might be said to be closer to James Buchanan's than to Friedrich Hayek's.[5] Additionally, the late Iberian scholastics were for the most part confident that the faculties of human reason went as far as allowing for the moral and ethical foundations of the proper political organization of the commonwealth to be rationally understood and applied.[6]

In other respects – particularly law – the late Iberian scholastics incorporated evolutionary elements in their analysis. In the context of his discussion of the *ius gentium*, Suárez provides an account of the relationship between custom and human law that will be particularly interesting for those familiar with Hayek's conception of law. Notwithstanding being human law, the *ius gentium* is not man made law, at least not in the sense of being deliberately designed by any human legislator. It is, for Suárez, 'obviously unwritten law' that is introduced not by mandate of any human legislator but 'by the habits and conduct not of one people or another but of the whole world.'[7] Perhaps the most relevant aspect of this account, is that it is a conception of law that is unwritten, custom-based, evolutionary and universal.

For reasons that should be obvious in the context of the previous chapters of this book, grasping the ideas of the Salamanca School is also important for understanding the history of Latin America and – of course – the Iberian Peninsula.[8] But, not withstanding the more obvious and direct connection with these regions, the contemporary relevance of the Salamanca School is not limited to the history of Spain, Portugal and their overseas colonies. In addition to fostering an unprecedented expansion of Christianity, the Iberian empires of the time of the Salamanca School also provided what can be described as the first true wave of globalization with deep implications not only on the economic, but also on the cultural and political domains.[9] Through the spread of their ideas (and of reactions against their ideas) in Europe and in other parts of the world, understanding the contributions of the late Iberian scholastics is also important for understanding world history in general.

In addition to the points already mentioned, it's important to emphasize that the late Iberian scholastics' theories of politics and law incorporate ample and well developed economic insights. This is at the root of the integrated approach to political philosophy and political economy that is made evident in their treatment of the ethics of (broadly defined) market activity.

## Political Economy and the Ethical Foundations of the Market

As rightfully pointed out by Barry (2003), the authors of the Salamanca School were able to anticipate many of the economic concepts and theories which later became central to the defence of free markets from the eighteenth century onwards. Schumpeter himself – in his monumental *History of Economic Analysis* – despite some notable flaws and omissions in his analysis of late scholasticism, recognized Molina as one of the most important contributors to economic thought of his period.[10] As expounded in Chapter 2 of this book, the Salamanca School provided important – and in some instances truly path-breaking – contributions in domains ranging from the understanding of value and the role of market prices to banking and monetary theory. Even on the subject of usury and interest – where the contributions of the late Iberian scholastics may seem less relevant from a contemporary perspective – they nevertheless in some aspects paved the way for later advances.[11] However, the increasingly recognized role of the late Iberian scholastics in the history of economic thought is not the only reason for their relevance in the context of contemporary political economy.

Another important aspect of the Salamanca School's approach to political economy is its close integration of ethics and economics. For the late Iberian scholastics, the analysis of the workings of the market could not be separated from a natural-law framework within which property and trade had clear and legitimate roles. Contemporary economic analysis often shies away from normative judgements and on dealing with many specific issues there are probably good reasons for doing so in order to minimize the risk of compromising the objectivity of the analysis. But from a more general perspective, an overall approach to political economy cannot ultimately subsist without sound ethical foundations and in this sense the late Iberian scholastics may be a very good example.[12] The works of the Salamanca School – despite the various shortcomings that may be identified in them from a contemporary standpoint – provide something that has become quite rare: a comprehensive perspective that combines natural law, ethics and economics in an integrated and consistent form.[13] For the late Iberian scholastics, the ultimate (analytical) aim of resolving moral issues required rational and objective analysis of economic processes in the context of natural law. And this in turn required a logically solid and anthropologically realistic analysis of human action.[14]

But perhaps the contributions of the late Iberian scholastics that are most relevant for contemporary political economy are those observed by Hayek, namely their early understanding of the market as a mechanism for coordinating decentralized knowledge and their insights into the workings of spontaneous order. In his Nobel Prize lecture, Hayek (1974) made clear the contemporary relevance he attributed to these authors:

> Indeed, the chief point was already seen by those remarkable anticipators of modern economics, the Spanish schoolmen of the sixteenth century, who emphasized that what they called *pretium mathematicum*, the mathematical price, depended on so many particular circumstances that it could never be known to man but was known only to God. I sometimes wish that our mathematical economists would take this to heart. I must confess that I still doubt whether their search for measurable magnitudes has made significant contributions to our theoretical understanding of economic phenomena – as distinct from their value as a description of particular situations.

By positing and explaining the existence of social phenomena that are of human origin but not of human design, the perspective of the late Iberian scholastics proved able to accommodate and contribute to resolve some of the most complex issues of political economy. In light of the perplexities and sterility of a significant portion of contemporary research in economics, perhaps it is not unreasonable to suggest that it is worth revisiting the ideas of the Salamanca School for more than the (laudable) goal of understanding the history of economic thought.

## Contemporary Catholic Social Thought

The approach and framework employed by the late Iberian scholastics make the ideas of the Salamanca School particularly relevant to contemporary Christian – and particularly Catholic – social thought. The relationship between Christian social thought and the market economy has traditionally been complex and often equivocal. While the fundamental principles of Catholic doctrine are not in any way at odds with a properly structured market economy, the truth is that there is a long and unfortunate history of mutually hostile views between some Christian social thinkers and defenders of free markets.[15] While a growing number of Christians have come to recognize the practical benefits of the market economy in terms of productivity and efficiency, the workings of the market are often accepted (or even tolerated) only under serious, and frequently misguided, reservations and caveats. This happens due to the perception of a wide range of ethical shortcomings in the workings of the market. While these judgements are often inaccurate, the frequent failure of libertarians and free-market conservatives to put forth a consistent ethical defence of the market ends up fuelling precisely the worst and most dangerous kind of ethical objections.

While the problem outlined exists in Christian social thought in general, it has been made more serious in Catholic social teaching by the popularity of Weber's well known thesis about the relationship between Protestantism and capitalism. This has reinforced the anti-capitalistic inclinations of many Catholics while simultaneously fostering the anti-Catholic sentiments of many defenders of the market economy. In this context, recalling and understanding the ideas of the authors of the Salamanca School – who were both committed Catholics and keen theorists of the economic and social order – is certainly helpful to dispel (or at least relativize) what Hayek described as the 'Weberian myth of the Protestant source of capitalist ethics'.[16]

The Salamanca School is also important in the context of the fortunate resurgence of interest in studies that aim at properly framing the market economy in the context of Christian social thought.[17] If one seeks to develop and consolidate an approach that combines Christian principles and doctrine with solid ethical and philosophical analysis of the market economy and the rule of law, then a proper understanding of the main insights of the late Iberian scholastics is indispensable. In fact, even for non-Christians (and non-believers) this should be a topic of interest, given that the worldwide Christian population is estimated at around two billion people and that the teachings of the Salamanca School may also be relevant for engaging in fruitful dialogue with adherents to other religions of Abrahamic origin.

Perhaps the best contemporary statement of a view that puts forth a correct understanding of the market economy within the framework of Catholic social thought is provided by Pope John Paul II in his 1991 encyclical *Centesimus Annus*, where, seeking to answer the question of whether capitalism is the social system that ought to be recommended in order to achieve true economic and civil progress, it is stated:

> If by 'capitalism' is meant an economic system which recognizes the fundamental and positive role of business, the market, private property and the resulting responsibility for the means of production, as well as free human creativity in the economic sector, then the answer is certainly in the affirmative, even though it would perhaps be more appropriate to speak of a 'business economy', 'market economy' or simply 'free economy'. But if by 'capitalism' is meant a system in which freedom in the economic sector is not circumscribed within a strong juridical framework which places it at the service of human freedom in its totality, and which sees it as a particular aspect of that freedom, the core of which is ethical and religious, then the reply is certainly negative.

This is very much the underlying view that was already present in the works of the Salamanca School and while it may perhaps be regarded by some as a weak defence of the market, it has the potential to be extremely robust given its integration of theological, ethical, juridical and economic insights. Like in the case of the specific provisions and exceptions allowed to the general rules of property in cases of extreme need, the integration into a broader ethical framework has the potential both to undermine general principles or – if properly interpreted – to solidify acceptance and respect for private property and its essential social function.[18] While some will probably always look at the integrated ethical, political and economic outlook of the Salamanca School as too demanding or as weakening the case for individual and economic liberty, for many others – both Christian and non-Christian – it has the potential to provide a defence of the market economy and the rule of law on firmer and more satisfying normative grounds.

Furthermore, in a contemporary context where there is often a trend towards political centralization of power, the strong emphasis of the late Iberian scholastics on the principle of subsidiarity provides a solid foundation for the defence of self-government and local and individual rights, while at the same time affirming the importance of the social bonds of family and community.

Last, but not least, in the context of religious thought and practice, the teachings of the Salamanca School and their application in the New World also provide an important example for addressing many of the problems of the contemporary world that are associated with attempts to impose by force particular ideologies or religions.[19] Indeed, the ideas of the Salamanca School are at least as relevant in the international sphere as in domestic affairs.

## International Relations and War

The teachings of the Salamanca School are also relevant to broader contemporary debates on international affairs. Sally (2008, p. 6) is justified in identifying the oldest arguments favouring unfettered free trade with the Christian tradition and naming Vitoria and Suárez in this regard. Nevertheless, the main arguments for both sides on contemporary debates on immigration and international trade can already, to a significant extent, be found in the works of the late Iberian scholastics. Diverging from the strongly libertarian stances of Vitoria (which are also the more representative of the Salamanca School as a whole),[20] Molina offers a set of arguments that would fit into a contemporary conservative defence of restrictions on international trade and/or immigration:

> ... the state or its governor can rightfully forbid to all foreigners the use of the country's possessions which are the joint property of all its citizens, provided that the foreigners have no urgent or serious need of them. ... Following on the division of lands and goods, the country's common possessions over which the entire community has control are just as much its own belongings as the personal possessions of the individual citizens are their own belongings. ... All the more may a country refuse trade, harbour facilities and residence to foreigners when it sees that such will add to their power, for it may rightly fear (human nature being what it is) that they will conquer the country or that it will suffers some other disadvantage from their trade and their presence. ... Because a country grants some foreigners access to some of its possessions it does not automatically lose its freedom to refuse similar access to other visitors, for everybody has the unimpaired right to allow the use of his possessions to whom he pleases, and refuse it to others.[21]

While contrasting the arguments put forth by Vitoria and Molina it is hard not to be reminded of contemporary debates on immigration, both across different ideological lines and even between contemporary authors who share libertarian credentials.[22]

On the subject of the use of force, the late Iberian scholastics were certainly not pacifists but at the same time they believed that the use of force was not outside the domain of moral judgement. A moral right to self-defence to protect both life and property was strongly affirmed and war was deemed an important topic for moral scrutiny. They recognized (and elaborated upon) a range of just causes for war (which in some cases might even be legitimate offensive war) and also debated thoroughly on the just conduct of war, including concepts like (what we would now refer to as) acceptable 'collateral damage'.[23]

The strong stances of the Salamanca School against wars aimed at converting pagans to Christianity also bear important teachings for contemporary debates on the best methods for the international promotion of liberal democracy and 'nation building' efforts. Although they regarded the conversion of pagans to Christianity as a moral imperative, the late Iberian scholastics generally opposed the use of coercion for such purposes both on normative and practical grounds.[24] Persuasion – not coercion – was the morally favoured method because only voluntary conversions could be regarded as sincere and truthful. At the same time, attempts to justify war against pagans on the need to facilitate their conversion were also condemned on practical grounds since military aggression would generate bad will against Christians and (quite rightly and rationally) lead pagans to resist and possibly retaliate. While in the contemporary world arguments for the legitimacy of wars to spread Christianity are not usually heard, these insights continue to be pertinent when applied to a range of ideologies and beliefs.[25]

## Concluding Remarks

The previous chapters of this book have shown how the Salamanca School contributed to a wide range of political, ethical and economic subjects making use of an integrated natural-law approach. While it would be inadequate to describe the late Iberian scholastics as either 'libertarian' or 'conservative' in the contemporary meaning of these labels, many of their insights may be said to bear special interest for these currents of political philosophy.

At a general level, the Salamanca School provided an account of the relationship between state, individuals and civil society that is in several ways responsive to some of the central concerns of contemporary libertarian and conservative thought. While neither the Dominican nor the Jesuit late Iberian scholastics can be described as individualists in the contemporary sense, their works exhibit a striking concern with personal dignity and rights while focusing on individual agency.[26]

Grasping the ideas of the Salamanca School is, most obviously, essential for gaining a proper understanding of the history and evolution of Western political and economic thought, but it is also – as has been made clear – a source of relevant insights for contemporary issues in their own right. In addition to being a powerful antidote against claims about the alleged incompatibility between Christianity and the market economy, the ideas of the Salamanca School also provide a glimpse of an alternative approach to modernity. This was an approach that sought to accommodate traditional conceptions of the common good with the growing challenges of modernity in terms of pluralism, individual rights, and the complexity of market activity, all within a natural-law framework. While the approach of the Salamanca School did not ultimately prevail, important elements were carried forth and helped give shape (directly or indirectly) to the ideas of subsequent authors and schools of thought. Despite the best attempts and theoretical contributions of the late Iberian scholastics, their ideas proved incapable of reversing the secularist and positivist tide that ultimately culminated in the French Revolution and is at the root of most contemporary forms of socialism. Nevertheless, studying the rich depository of ideas of the Salamanca School offers the possibility of recovering important insights on a wide range subjects and – perhaps more crucially – suggests a possible alternative programme for a consistent and sustainable defence of well-ordered liberty in the contemporary world.

# Notes

## Chapter 1

[1] Hayek (1974).
[2] Pribram (1983) and Chafuen (2003).
[3] The 1874 book by Wilhelm Endemann is *Studien in der romanisch-kanonistischen Wirtschafts und Rechtslehre bis gegen Ende des 16 Jahrhunderts*. Cited by Grice-Hutchinson (1993), p. 24. For an analysis of the evolution of the usage of the name 'School of Salamanca' see Grice-Hutchinson (1993), pp. 23–25.
[4] Termes (1999), p. 32.
[5] On these innovations, which also involved the generalization of Metaphysics as an autonomous teaching subject in Spanish and Portuguese universities, see Saranyana (2007), pp. 484–489.
[6] Montes (1998), p. 40.
[7] Montes (1998), p. 29.
[8] This is the position of Henry Kamen in his *Una Sociedad conflictiva: España, 1469–1714*, Madrid: Alianza, 1989, pp. 247–252. The author notes that the learned elite proceeded chiefly from the three main Universities of Castilla: Salamanca, Valladolid and Alcalá. For example, of the 103 judges nominated by the *Real Chancillería* de Valladolid between 1588 and 1633, only seven had not attended one of these three Universities. Cited in Montes (1998), p. 29.
[9] For an extended overview and discussion of these and other factors, see Montes (1998), pp. 26–41.
[10] Montes (1998), pp. 30–32.
[11] Ozment (1980), pp. 397–398.
[12] Ozment (1980), pp. 407–409. The Council of Trent is considered to have been one of the most important Ecumenical Council of the Catholic Church. It convened in Trento (now part of Italy) and its main outcomes were a number of Church reforms, a restatement of catholic teachings on a number of doctrinal areas and

the condemnation of several central Protestant claims as heresies. The Council of Trent is therefore usually regarded as the main symbol of the Counter-Reformation, a movement in which the teachings of late Iberian scholastics played a key role.

[13] Papal bulls are specific written and authenticated documents issued by the popes with their most important utterances. Usage of the term has had some historical variation but is now generally used to refer only to the most formal papal documents, usually stating positions that are deemed sufficiently important to justify this form of communication.

[14] Höpfl (2004), pp. 8–9.

[15] Montes (1998), pp. 33–34.

[16] Although Pagden (2002, p. 84) overstates when he claims that at the time no one 'really understood the mechanisms of inflation'; as is shown in Chapter 2 of this book this was far from being the case. Some of the late Iberian scholastics showed a clear understanding of the basic causes of inflation and provided clear warnings about its likely consequences. Unfortunately, as often happened in history, their teachings insufficient to change course and prevent economic problems.

[17] Haldane (2004, p. 125). On the decline of scholastic economics, see Roover (1955, pp. 171–177).

[18] See Chapter 3 of this book.

[19] See Burke (2006).

[20] For a more developed biographical summary see Hamilton (1963, pp. 171–176).

[21] Saranyana (2007), pp. 452–455.

[22] '*Relectiones*' were public lectures usually given once a year that summarized the content of a course.

[23] See Vitoria (1991) for contemporary English translations of his political writings.

[24] Saranyana (2007, pp. 457–459); Grice-Hutchinson (1978, p. 94). For additional biographical information see Hamilton (1963, pp. 176–180) and the more detailed account in Carro (1968, pp. xix–xxvi).

[25] Domingo de Soto's *Deliberación en la causa de los pobres*, published in 1545 in Salamanca is particularly noteworthy in this domain. See Saranyana (2007, pp. 460–461).

[26] Grice-Hutchinson (1978, p. 95); Juana (2007, pp. 3–4).

[27] Grice-Hutchinson (1978, p. 118). For a modern English translation see Azpilcueta (2007).

[28] See Pereña Vicente (1957) and Melody (1908) for additional biographical information on Diogo de Covarrubias y Leyva. Fernandéz-Santamaria (1977, pp. 87–88) describes Covarrubias as 'the figure

reigning supreme over the Salmantine jurists' and 'the age's most influential Spanish legal mind'.
29 Saranyana (2007), p. 490.
30 For further contextualization of Mercado's contributions in his *Suma*, see the introductory study by R. Sierra Bravo to Mercado (1975). For an English translation of an extract from Mercado's *Suma* see Grice-Hutchinson (1952), pp. 96–103.
31 Beltrán (1989), pp. 40–41.
32 See Galindo Garcia (1999).
33 Grice-Hutchinson (1978), p. 97; see also Saranyana (2007), p. 491.
34 The *encomienda* was a system whereby the colonizers were given responsibility and power over a group of natives whom they were supposed to educate and convert to Christianity and from whom they could demand tribute. In practice, although not in theory, Amerindians were subject to condition of near serfdom under the rule of Spanish *encomenderos*. For more on Las Casas' activism against the *encomienda* system, see Chapter 3 of this book.
35 Watner (1987, pp. 298–300); Bandelier (1908). Fernández (1971) provides a detailed biographical account.
36 Hamilton (1963, pp. 180–184); Pohle (1911).
37 See Molina (1988) for a recent English translation of Part IV of the *Concordia*.
38 The reception and impact of the *Concordia* is better understood in light of the heated controversies of the time on the relationship between freedom, (divine) foreknowledge and predestination. These were largely ignited by the positions taken by Pope Pius V in 1567 against the thesis of the theologian Miguel Bayo (1513–1589) and often resulted in confrontations between Dominicans against Jesuits in subsequent years. See Saranyana (2007, pp. 467–469) and Moreira (1992).
39 Such is the content of Mariana's later works that Huerta de Soto (1999) goes as far as stating that the Jesuit Father Juan de Mariana was possibly 'the most libertarian of all the scholastics, particularly in his later works'.
40 Lehmkuhl (1910).
41 Béltran (1996), pp. 255–266.
42 Saranyana (2007), pp. 469–470; Hamilton (1963, pp. 184–188).
43 Pérez Goyena (1912).
44 For an outline of the main issues in Suárez 54 *disputationes*, see Saranyana (2007), pp. 470–478.
45 Pérez Goyena (1912).
46 Skinner (1978), p. 138.
47 This topic is developed in Chapter 3 of this book.

## Chapter 2

1. Rommen (1945, p. 543).
2. For more developed summaries of his life and works, see McDermott (1993), focusing more on Aquinas' philosophical writings, and Dyson (2002), particularly on Aquinas' political thought.
3. McDermott (1993, p. xv).
4. Fortin (1987, p. 248).
5. See Hamilton (1963, pp. 4–5 and 11–12) and also the next section of the present chapter.
6. See Dyson (2002, pp. xxxii–xxxv).
7. See *Summa Theologiae* IaIIae, q. 94, a. 2. The quotation uses the translation in Aquinas (2002, pp. 117–118). On reason and law in Aquinas see also Brett (1997, pp. 95–97).
8. Human laws which bear a close proximity with the principles of natural law and therefore apply to all peoples are sometimes referred to by the scholastics as the *ius gentium* (the law of peoples or law of nations). Although the meaning of the term varies somewhat between authors and contexts, it usually refers to an intermediate notion between natural law and positive human law.
9. Dyson (2002, p. xxxiv).
10. Fortin (187, p. 252).
11. For an assessment of Aquinas' synthesis of ethics and moral theology in the context of Medieval and Renaissance ethics see Haldane (2004, pp. 115–125).
12. Nominalism is the doctrine in metaphysics that holds that universals have no existence beyond particulars. Nominalists hold that general terms or names do exist (hence the term 'nominalism') but that universals have no definite existence apart from the particular objects to which they are applied.
13. There are however good reasons to believe that Aquinas' *Summa Theologica* had already been gradually assuming the position of basic textbook in the schools of the Dominican Order well before the same shift took place in the Universities; see Brett (1997, pp. 103 and 125).
14. Skinner (1978, pp. 135–136); Haldane (2004, p. 6).
15. Burns (2006, p. 153).
16. Burns (2006, pp. 153–154) for example, in the context of discussing the European Thomist revival, states: 'In the third quarter of the sixteenth century, however, the most important and creative Thomist thinking was done neither in Italy nor in France but in Spain.'
17. Hamilton (1963, p. 173).

[18] Rommen (1948, p. 440).
[19] Gierke (1987, p. 81) is somewhat hyperbolic in his description but his central idea that in 'this sense Medieval Doctrine was already filled with the thought of the inborn and indestructible rights of the Individual' seems hard to deny. See subsection in this chapter on 'Individual rights and the common good' for more on the late Iberian scholastics' approach to individual rights.
[20] A similar point is made in Hamilton (1963, p. 5).
[21] Skinner refers here primarily to Molina, Suárez and Domingo de Soto but the point has broader validity.
[22] The contrast between Augustinian and Thomist approaches on this issue is emphasised by Dyson (2007, p. xxix).
[23] See section on 'The Ethical and Juridical Framewok of the Market' in this chapter for an overview of the main contributions to political economy of the Salamanca School.
[24] There has for a long time (and for a range of different reasons) been considerable controversy over the adequacy of the expressions 'Protestant Reformation' and 'Catholic Counter Reformation'. They are used here simply because they are the most widely established terms and so are more likely to facilitate comprehension. On the controversy see, for example, Ozment (1980, pp. 397–398).
[25] Oakley (2006, p. 164).
[26] See Ozment (1980, pp. 398–402) for an overview of the main issues and disputations that eventually led to the Council of Trent.
[27] Ozment (1980, p. 402).
[28] See Ozment (1980, pp. 406–409).
[29] On this view and its theological-political implications see Oakley (2006, pp. 164–175).
[30] Ozment (1980, p. 407).
[31] See Loyola (1989) for a contemporary English translation. As Ignatius of Loyola (1989, p. 47) himself described the purpose of the Exercises 'is to help the exercitant to conquer himself, and to regulate his life so that he will not be influenced in his decisions by any inordinate attachment'.
[32] See Höpfl (2004, pp. 8–9).
[33] On the early Jesuits' peculiar combination of obedience to hierarchy and rules, self-mastery and abilities to exercise autonomous judgement see Höpfl (2004, pp. 26–35).
[34] For more on the influence of the Salamanca School on the Counter-Reformation see Chapter 3.
[35] Brett (1997, p. 1).
[36] Hamilton (1963, 30).

37 See Skinner (1978, 155–156) for a short summary of the views of Domingo de Soto, Francisco de Vitoria, Francisco Suárez and Luis de Molina on this topic and Pereña Vicente (1957) for a thorough discussion of the ideas of Diego de Covarrubias y Leyva.
38 See Brett (1997, 137–164) for a detailed exposition and discussion of Domingo de Soto's contribution in this regard.
39 Domingo de Soto (1968 [1556]), book v, q. i, a. vii. (our translation) This passage is also discussed in Hamilton (1963, 30–31) and Brett (1997, 160–161).
40 See Höpfl (2004, 284–287) for a summary of generally accepted limitations of individual rights justified by the common good.
41 See Höpfl (2004, 292–296).
42 The utilitarian flavour of some of the arguments for property is rooted in the fact that property rights were regarded as not being directly derived from natural law. See Höpfl (2004, 301–306) and Chafuen (2003, 31–50). This topic is addressed in more detail below.
43 See Pereña Vicente (1957).
44 Gierke (1987, p. 45).
45 See for example Skinner (1978, pp. 148–149) and section on 'Philosophical and Political Foundations of the School' in this chapter for contextualization of the Thomist natural law framework.
46 Vitoria (1991, pp. 10–11).
47 See Brett (1997, p. 136).
48 See Pagden and Lawrence (1991, pp. xix–xx). Against the notion that Vitoria provides an early formulation of social contract theory, see Fernandéz-Santamaria (1977, pp. 72–73).
49 See Skinner (1978, pp. 155–157) on the use by the late scholastics of the concept of the state of nature as a starting point in the process of explaining the establishment of political society. Höpfl (2004, p. 231) disagrees with Skinner stressing that the concept was rarely used and had a different meaning from that in the works of Hobbes and Locke.
50 See Fernandéz-Santamaria (1977, pp. 65–69).
51 See Skinner (1978, pp. 158–166).
52 Mariana goes even further in dissociating himself from Thomist tradition and in some instances postulates an account of life in pre-political society that is close to being Hobbesian. See Höpfl (2004, pp. 239–248) and Braun (2007, pp. 16–26).
53 It's worth recalling that while the legitimacy of the *establishment* of the state was to be judged by the standard of consent (even if only tacit), the legitimacy of the actual *exercise* of political power was – as

already stressed above – to be evaluated primarily by its accordance with natural law.
54 While the overall point on concern is accepted, Skinner's (1978, p. 161) direct identification of the Thomist approach with Rousseau is certainly disputable. Rommen (1948, p. 449) stresses the continuity of this approach since Aquinas to Suárez and argues that 'Only a superficial comparison of words without the logical systematic framework and the determined meaning could lead to the notion that Suarez' theory is a forerunner of Rousseau's "contrat social."'
55 See Höpfl (2004, pp. 248–253) for an overview of Suárez use of contractual language and concepts.
56 See Höpfl (2004, pp. 256–257 and 261–262).
57 Suárez' emphasis on the precedence of the common good and the dominant position in which his conception of the pactum places the ruler led Lloyd (2006, pp. 296–297) to summarize his thought as oriented 'towards the supremacy and licensed encroachment of the public over and upon the private sphere at the behest of the monarch's will – and so towards absolutism', this in spite of recognizing that Suárez 'accommodated significant elements of the constitutionalist tradition.' While there were certainly elements of tension and even incoherence in Suárez' political thought it is rather far fetched to position him as paving the way to absolutism.
58 Salmon (2006, pp. 238–239).
59 Cited in Hamilton (1963, p. 62). On Suárez' approach to legitimate deposition and tyrannicide, see also Höpfl (2004, pp. 332–337).
60 See Skinner (1978, pp. 177–178).
61 See Hamilton (1963, pp. 63–64).
62 See Braun (2007, pp. 79–91).
63 Quoted in Braun (2007, p. 90).
64 In comparing the generally more cautious Suárez with Mariana, Höpfl (2004, p. 257) concludes that Suárez 'could not resist Mariana's logic that the public assembly of the commonwealth is the appropriate agent for disciplining kings, and that tyrannicide was the *ultima ratio.*'
65 See Hamilton (1963, p. 114).
66 Locke (1990, pp. 63–64): 'Again: that Church can have no right to be tolerated by the magistrate, which is constituted upon such a bottom, that all those who enter into it, do thereby, *ipso facto*, deliver themselves up to the protection and service of another prince. For by this means the magistrate would give way to the settling of a foreign jurisdiction in his own country, and suffer his own people to be listed, as it were, for soldiers against his own government.

Nor does the frivolous and fallacious distinction between the court and the church afford any remedy to this inconvenience; especially when both the one and the other are equally subject to the absolute authority of the same person, who has not only power to persuade the members of his Church to whatsoever he lists, either as purely religious, or in order thereunto, but can also enjoin it them on pain of eternal fire. . . . Lastly, those are not at all to be tolerated who deny the being of a God. Promises, covenants, and oaths, which are the bonds of human society, can have no hold upon an atheist. The taking away of God, though but even in thought, dissolves all. Besides also, those that by their atheism undermine and destroy all religion, can have no pretence of religion whereupon to challenge the privilege of a toleration.'

[67] See Hamilton (1963, pp. 110–113).
[68] See Hamilton (1963, pp. 116–119).
[69] See Höpfl (2004, pp. 133–139).
[70] See Vitoria (1991, pp. 45–151) and also the summarized analysis in Pagden and Lawrence (1991, pp. xxi–xxiii).
[71] See Hamilton (1963, pp. 73–75).
[72] See Hamilton (1963, pp. 76–82).
[73] See Rommen (1945, pp. 547–548).
[74] Vitoria (1991, pp. 90–91) does however recognize special instances where civil power may be subject to spiritual power, specifically if the actions of the civil policy are 'detrimental to the spiritual ministry'. On this topic, see also Hamilton (1963, pp. 84–88).
[75] Salmon (2006, p. 240).
[76] See Braun (2007, p. 88).
[77] Domingo de Soto (1968 [1556]), book iv, q. iv, a. i. (our translation).
[78] See Hamilton (1963, p. 61).
[79] See Rommen (1945, pp. 620–621). On the concept of *ius gentium* within the framework of natural law, see subsection on 'Thomism and natural law' in this chapter.
[80] Hamilton (1963, p. 98) classifies as absurd the attempts to credit either the late Iberian scholastics or Grotius with being the founders of international law, but this judgement appears to be founded on a too narrow understanding of modern international law as dealing 'mostly with the application and interpretation of treaties between sovereign states'. If a more general approach to international law is taken, the importance of the contributions of the Salamanca School – as well as those of Grotius – becomes more readily apparent. See Scott (1934) for the classic argument in favour of regarding Vitoria as the founder of international law.

81 See Hamilton (1963, pp. 99–102). For an overview of Diego de Covarrubias' specific perspective on the relationship between slavery and the *ius gentium*, see Pereña Vicente (1957, pp. 165–166). Covarrubias considered that the same civilizational principles that led to the institution of slavery as a legitimate form of dealing with enemy prisoners taken in a just war might equally lead – at a later historical stage – to the suppression of slavery as a method of coercion. He in fact regarded the (at the time) consolidating custom that Christian prisoners could not be made slaves even in the context of a just war as a sign of the evolutionary nature of a framework of international law founded upon the *ius gentium*.
82 See Hamilton (1962, pp. 103–104).
83 See Höpfl (2004, pp. 303–304).
84 See Fernandéz-Santamaria (1977, pp. 97–100).
85 On Suárez, see Höpfl (2004, pp. 304–306) and Hamilton (1963, pp. 106–109).
86 See Pereña Vicente (1957, pp. 168–178). For the roughly similar stances of Vitoria, Soto, Molina and Suárez on this regard, see Hamilton (1963, pp. 135–137).
87 See also Hamilton (1963, pp. 137–140) and Fernandéz-Santamaria (1977, p. 90).
88 Individuals may legitimately defend their persons and property from immediate danger but they may not avenge wrongs suffered, punish aggressors or recover stolen property by force once it has been taken way. For these purposes, private persons must present their cases to a judge.
89 See Fernandéz-Santamaria (1977, pp. 91–92) and also Hamilton (1963, pp. 142–143), where it is pointed out that Suárez went as far as refuting the savagery of pagans as a legitimate reason for war by asserting that 'this argument cannot be applied generally, because it is obvious that many pagans are more talented than Christians and more suited to political life.'
90 Rommen (1949, p. 549).
91 See Hamilton (1963, pp. 145–147).
92 See Rommen (1949, pp. 657–658). Although, according to Vitoria (1991, p. 299) if it's a matter of self-defence and no other course of action is available: 'Any person, even a private citizen, may declare and wage defensive war.'
93 See Rommen (1949, pp. 665–667).
94 It should be mentioned that Victoria is somewhat more affirmative on this regard than Molina. See Hamilton (1963, pp. 152–155).
95 See Hamilton (1963, pp. 150–152).

[96] As noted by Fernandéz-Santamaria (1977, p. 137), Erasmus suggestion of granting impunity to evildoers in order to protect the innocent was out of the question, for the 'result, argue the Spanish doctors unanimously, would be to further encourage the rapacity of the lawless and so plunge humanity into further chaos'.

[97] See Moreira (1999, pp. 84–86). For a very useful survey of primary and secondary sources see Rivas (1999).

[98] See subsection on 'Individual rights and the common good' above.

[99] On the utilitarian arguments employed to justify private property by the Salamanca School, see also Zaratiegui (2000).

[100] On the relationship between Catholic doctrine and attitudes towards poverty and private property, see Moreira (1996, particularly pp. 150–152).

[101] Gierke (1987, p. 80).

[102] Domingo de Soto (1968 [1556]), book i, q. v, a. iv. (our translation).

[103] Domingo de Soto (1968 [1556]), book iv, q. iii, a. i. (our translation). The entire third question (with only one article) is a defence of private property and a refutation of the arguments advanced in favour of common ownership. Hamilton (1963, p. 101) erroneously refers to this question as being from book iii when it is in fact from book iv.

[104] Quoted in Chafuen (2003, pp. 34–35).

[105] See Chafuen (2003, pp. 33–38) for additional examples.

[106] See Zaratiegui (2000, p. 92).

[107] Quoted in Hamilton (1963, p. 32).

[108] See Chafuen (2003, pp. 73–74).

[109] See Chafuen (2003, pp. 74–76) and subsection on 'Church and state' in this chapter, where the diverging views of Vitoria (who was a strong advocate of free trade) and Molina are described.

[110] For a more thorough analysis of the topic, see Chafuen (2003, pp. 42–45).

[111] Quoted in Chafuen (2003, p. 44).

[112] In fact, the distortions and misconceptions often reach further back by attributing Aquinas a definite or implicit labour theory of value and even picturing him as a precursor of Marxism. See Roover (1958, pp. 421–423) for an analysis and refutation of these claims.

[113] See Grice-Hutchinson (1978, p. 98) and Roover (1958, p. 424).

[114] Quoted in Grice-Hutchinson (1978, p. 100).

[115] Molina (1981, p. 160, our translation from Spanish).

[116] For more on the relationship between just price, legal price, natural price and common estimation, see Chafuen (2003, pp. 85–88).

[117] See Chafuen (2003, pp. 88–89).

[118] See Roover (1958, p. 426) who considers this to be a 'weakness' of the scholastic doctors for failing to recognize the necessity of price controls in at least some circumstances. However, if one regards price controls as ultimately ineffective this should be classified as an additional strength of the economic analysis of the Salamanca School.

[119] The three reasons are inter-connected: because money in itself was regarded as non-productive and no one could profit solely from time, charging interest on a money loan was like selling a perishable good (like wine or wheat) and simultaneously charging a fee for the right to use that good. One could legitimately charge a fee for the use of a non-perishable good (such as rent for the use of a house or a vineyard) but not for non-productive goods such as money was considered to be. See Aquinas (2002, particularly pp. 220–225).

[120] See Grice-Hutchinson (1978) for an overview of medieval practices to conceal the charging of interest on money loans.

[121] See Aquinas (2002, particularly pp. 225–229).

[122] As mentioned by Roover in the text that figures as the introduction to Cajetan (2007, p. 204): 'Cajetan's treatise helped to lift the barriers that still opposed the march of capitalism.' See also Rothbard (2006, pp. 99–101) on 'Cardinal Cajetan: the liberal Thomist' and Chafuen (2003, p. 124) on Cajetan's implicit use of time preference to justify the payment of interest.

[123] Chafuen (2003, p. 120).

[124] See Wood (2002, p. 204) and Gregg (2008, pp. 76–77).

[125] See Chafuen (2003, pp. 121 and 124–125)

[126] Somewhat ironically, as noted by Wood (2002, p. 205) it was the comparably unsophisticated analysis of Protestant thinkers that ended fuelling the controversy over usury in the following decades: 'it was the Protestants, with their biblically based faith, who kept the usury debate alive by returning to the traditional scholastic principles.'

[127] Huerta de Soto (2006, p. 78). The most complete and integrated analysis of the theories of banking of the Salamanca School can be found in Huerta de Soto (2006, pp. 78–97 and 603–612). See Huerta de Soto (1996) for an earlier version of the first section.

[128] Under a fractional-reserve system, banks in effect create money, subject to the reserve ratios imposed by the public authority. Some of the main economists of the Austrian School – such as Ludwig von Mises, Murray N. Rothbard and Jesús Huerta de Soto, argue that fractional-reserve banking is one of the causes of boom and bust cycles and defend 100 per cent reserve banking as an alternative.

[129] See Huerta de Soto (2006, pp. 93–97) and also Chafuen (2003, p. 123).
[130] Quoted in Huerta de Soto (2006, pp. 96–97).
[131] See Huerta de Soto (2006, pp. 84–90).
[132] For more on earlier contributions, see Grice-Hutchinson (1978). Chafuen (2003, pp. 61–71) offers an excellent overall summary of the late Iberian scholastics' theory of money, although the analysis would have benefited from further consideration of and integration with their theories of banking.
[133] See Huerta de Soto (2006, p. 603).
[134] Azpilcueta (2007, p. 70). The original text is from 1556. Despite Azpilcueta's notably clear statement of the main principle of the quantity theory of money, it's worth noting that the first person to state that theory was arguably Nicholas Copernicus in his earlier (1526) study *De monetae cudendae ratio more*, although in a less developed way than Azpilcueta. See Rothbard (2006, p. 165) and Huerta de Soto (2006, p. 604).
[135] Barry (2003, p. 44).
[136] For an extended presentation of this position and its implications, see Camacho (2007).
[137] Quoted in Camacho (2007, p. 120).
[138] See Chafuen (2003, pp. 63–65).
[139] Mariana (2007, p. 259): 'we grant the king the authority to debase money without the people's consent, in the pressing circumstances of war or siege – provided that the debasement is not extended beyond the time of need and, that when peace has been restored, he faithfully makes satisfaction to those who suffered loss'. It's worth noting that Mariana (2007, p. 304) was also certainly not of the opinion that popular consent made the debasement of currency unproblematic: 'If such is done, without consulting the people, it is unjust; if done with their consent, it is in many ways fatal.'
[140] Chafuen (2007, p. 243).
[141] His treatise on the alteration of money – *De monetae mutatione* – actually led to his imprisonment at the ripe age of 73, thus apparently proving that denouncing the government's inflationary policies might actually be more dangerous than writing at length about tyrannicide. See Rothbard (2006, pp. 119–122).
[142] Gregg (2008, p. 78).
[143] See Chafuen (2003, pp. 51–60).
[144] Domingo de Soto (1968 [1556]), book iii, q. vi, a. vii. (our translation). All the following quotes of Domingo de Soto are from this source.
[145] Suárez emphasized the same idea when he stressed that taxes imposed for particular projects must, in principle, be spent on those

projects, since 'if a [just] cause is necessary [for levying a tax], the tax cannot last longer than the cause.' Quoted in Höpfl (2004, p. 309).
146  See Höpfl (2004, p. 307).

# Chapter 3

1. For a biographical account of Las Casas and some of the other main figures of the School of Salamanca, see Chapter 1.
2. See Casas (1992 [ca. 1552]) for a contemporary English translation. As mentioned in the translator's preface to this edition (p. xxvi): 'Spelling and grammatical errors are not uncommon' and there is a clear excess of superlatives owing to the fact Bartolomé de Las Casas 'thinks in extremes, even in his grammar; he rarely uses one noun when two or three will serve the same task.' For an overview of Las Casa's vast literary output see Afanasiev (1971).
3. See Hanke (2002, p. 18).
4. See Hanke (2002, pp. 23–25).
5. See for example Las Casas (1971, 1992 and 2004).
6. Carro (1971) emphasizes basically the same point although from a perspective more sympathetic to the virtues of the Spanish monarchs of the period.
7. See Hanke (2002, pp. 42–53).
8. See Hanke (2002, pp. 54–71).
9. On this bull and its relationship with the debates over the status of the American Indians, see Hanke (1994, pp. 17–22). The bull *Sublimis Deus* followed the 1493 bull *Inter cetera*, where pope Alexander VI had granted exploration of the New World to Spain with the aim of converting the natives.
10. Quoted in Hanke (2002, pp. 72–73).
11. See Hanke (2002, pp. 77–81) and Biermann (1971).
12. Biermann (1971, p. 478) disagrees with Lewis Hanke's conclusion that the episode represented a failure of the Verapaz project of peaceful conversion, pointing out that Las Casas was opposed to wars to impose Spanish domination but not to wars of self-defence, as was the case of this conflict where 'the question was one of unprovoked attack by pagans on a land that had voluntarily placed itself under Spanish rule'.
13. On Las Casas and the New Laws of 1542, see Hanke (2002, pp. 83–105).
14. For a thorough treatment of the disputation between Las Casas and Sepúlveda, see Hanke (1994) and Losada (1971).

15. See Vitoria (1991, pp. 233–292).
16. See Vitoria (1991, pp. 251–277) for the unjust titles and Vitoria (1991, pp. 277–292) for the just titles. Useful summaries and discussion may be found in Fernandéz-Santamaria (1977, pp. 80–87) and Hamilton (1963, pp. 123–134).
17. On the declaration of war to unbelievers because of their lack of faith, Vitoria (1991, p. 272) states clearly: 'war is no argument for the truth of the Christian faith. Hence the barbarians cannot be moved by war to believe, but only to pretend that they believe and accept the Christian faith; and this is monstrous and sacrilegious.'
18. Hanke (1994, p. 67).
19. See Losada (1971, pp. 284–300) and Hanke (1994, pp. 83–99).
20. On the protection of the innocents against such practices it can be reasonably argued that it was Sepúlveda – and not Las Casas – who was in fact closer to Vitoria's position.
21. On Las Casas as a literary figure and his projection in popular culture, see Marcus (1971).
22. For a defence of Las Casas against his critics, see Comas (1971). For critical views on Las Casas, see Araujo (1995).
23. See Comas (1971, pp. 505–506) and Bataillon (1971, pp. 415–418).
24. Interestingly, Vitoria was one of the first to express concerns about the African slave trade and Molina later deemed the conditions of enslavement a topic of discussion. See Bataillon (1971, p. 418).
25. Castro (2007, p. 185).
26. While Las Casas was certainly motivated primarily by a sense of religious duty and regarded his actions as ultimately beneficial to the Spanish Crown, his portrayal as an agent of 'imperialism' inevitably strikes out as at least a somewhat anachronic reading of the historical facts.
27. The Catholic recovery, a process in which the recently formed Society of Jesus played a crucial role, was more significant in Bavaria, Hapsburg Austrian and Rhenish episcopacies. See Ozment (1980, pp. 416–418).
28. See Rommen (1945, pp. 544–545).
29. As pointed out by Rommen (1945, p. 554): 'The adversaries against whom the doctors of Late Scholasticism had to fight were the partisans of the rising absolute sovereignty of the national kings, who claimed not only the plenitude of temporal power but also sovereignty in the spiritual sphere and over the canon law.' The fact that many Protestant princes probably looked upon Luther's ideas as a practical means of consolidating their power through the establishment of national state churches certainly helped the ultimate triumph of the notion of the divine and absolute right of kings.

30 On Calvinist resistance theory, see Kingdon (2006), which includes a section on Lutheran resistance theory (pp. 200–203). See also Skinner (1978, p. 347) on the similarities between Mariana's and theory of political power and Calvinist thought. Rothbard (2006, pp. 135–175) is well worth reading for the analysis of the integration of Protestant political and economic thought of the period.

31 Skinner (1978, p. 163) is representative in his regard when he states that the analysis of the legitimate polity as being founded in a previous act of popular consent 'was carried to a new peak of development by the sixteenth-century Thomists, and in particular by Suárez, whose The Laws and God the Lawgiver may be said to have supplied the guidelines for the handling of the same theme by some of the leading constitutionalist writers of the seventeenth century.'

32 In addition to Vitoria, Reichberg et al. (2006) also include in their selection of readings, English translations of texts on war by Molina and Suárez.

33 See Chapter 2 of this book for an overview of the positions of the late Iberian scholastics on this topic.

34 Rommen (1945, p. 623).

35 See Brett (1997, pp. 165–204).

36 See Chafuen (2003, pp. 15–16). Although it may be liable to accusations of over-simplifying, the figure in Chafuen (2003, p. 16) is helpful in providing a visual representation of this process of diffusion of ideas. Grice-Hutchinson (1978, pp. 107–115) provides a useful account of the transmission of the theory of value of the late Iberian scholastics.

37 In fact Molina pursued most of his academic career in Portugal, and the Portuguese Universities of Coimbra and Évora were, at the time, major intellectual centres. Pedro de Fonseca was a specialist in Aristotle and broadly Thomist. He taught at Coimbra for most of his academic life and his metaphysics both influenced Suárez and in some respects anticipated Molina. See Saranyana (2007, pp. 487–489).

38 On Lessius and Juan de Lugo, see Rothbard (2006, pp. 122–127), who considers them the last Salamancans (Lessius in spirit only since he was born near Antwerp).

39 This theme is explored more in depth in Gordley (1991).

40 On Locke's opinions about the scholastics, see Grabill (2007, p. xix).

41 In a roughly similar line of reasoning but with a significant degree of hyperbolic excess, Lord Acton (1985, p. 71) argued that 'the greater part of the political ideas of Milton, Locke, and Rousseau, may be found in the ponderous Latin of Jesuits who were subjects of the Spanish Crown, of Lessius, Molina, Mariana, and Suarez.' On the

relationship between Locke and the Salamanca School, see Alves and Moreira (2009).

42. Roover (1955, pp. 188–189). It's also worth noting that the course in Moral Philosophy taught by Francis Hutcheson and later by Adam Smith shows evidence of an approach to economic principles closer to the tradition of the medieval university than to mercantilist thought, particularly in its integrated approach to ethics, law and economics.

43. See Grice-Hutchinson (1978, p. 108) and Roover (1955, p. 189).

44. See Rizo Patrón (2006, pp. 11–12). Among the professors of the University of San Marcos that studied at Salamanca were Pedro Gutiérrez Flores, Francisco León Garabito, and Alonso Velásquez. The influential Jesuit José de Acosta (1539–1600), who studied at the University of Alcalá but was heavily influenced by the School of Salamanca, also taught at the University of San Marcos, as did Francisco Carrasco del Saz (d. 1625) and Juan de Solórzano Pereira (1575–1655) who had also studied at Salamanca.

45. On later developments of scholasticism in Central and South American universities, see Saranyana (2007, pp. 502–504).

# Chapter 4

1. While theology was regarded as the ultimate aim in terms of knowledge, good theological reasoning was considered impossible in the absence of proper foundations in metaphysics and these in turn required sound philosophical reasoning. In other words, the desire the late Iberian scholastics to be good theologians constituted a powerful incentive to practice and develop philosophical knowledge and extend it to all relevant domains, among which politics (both domestic and international) and economics.

2. For a contemporary perspective that is critical of Molina's attempt to reconcile free will and divine grace through his theory of 'middle knowledge', see Kenny (1979). For a contemporary defence of the accuracy and relevance of Molina's views, see Freddoso (1988, particularly pp. 62–81).

3. See Saranyana (2007, pp. 469–471).

4. See Skinner (1978, pp. 248–249).

5. For an overview of the political thought of Hayek and Buchanan, see the volumes devoted to them in the same collection of which this book is part. For a comparative analysis of the Hayek's and Buchanan's approach to politics and also an overview of the authors that most influenced their political thought, see Alves (2006).

6 The idea that human reason is able to grasp objective reality and understand the structure of the natural order is carried forth in the works of twentieth century neo-Thomists such as the highly influential Jacques Maritain (see Haldane 2004, pp. 9–10). Although there are some important differences, this epistemological feature of the Salamanca School curiously bears important points of contact with the approaches of Ludwig von Mises, Murray N. Rothbard and Ayn Rand.
7 Quoted in Hamilton (1963, p. 107). The custom based nature of Suárez conception of the *ius gentium* is noted in Hamilton (1963, pp. 106–109), although less attention is paid to his evolutionary insights, which are arguably more relevant.
8 On Las Casas and the development of Latin American history in the United States, see Hanke (2002, pp. 219–243).
9 It is no coincidence that the origins of comparative ethnology can be traced back to this period and to the controversies over the New World in which the Salamanca School played a pivotal role. Pagden (1982, p. 146) notes that Las Casas provided the 'first detailed comparative analysis of Amerindian culture'.
10 Schumpeter (1994) was first published in 1954. Interestingly, Schumpeter (1994, p. 54) also noted the similarity between Carl Menger's subjective theory of value and the ideas of the late Iberian scholastics Molina and Lugo.
11 Despite some interesting insights on time preference and on helping pave the way for a wider acceptance of the payment of compensation for money loans, the contributions of the late Iberian scholastics on interest can be regarded as their less exciting from the point of view of contemporary libertarianism (although that may not necessarily be the case from some conservative perspectives). On this topic, see also Chafuen (2003, pp. 146–148).
12 On the need to make an ethical case for the market (even if only a fairly minimalistic one) and provide answers to ethical critiques of the free market, see Meadowcroft (2005).
13 See Chafuen (2003, pp. 24–26).
14 Perhaps the best exponent of this among the late Iberian scholastics is Juan de Mariana, whose keen insights into taxation, public expenditure and the workings of government make him a veritable precursor to public choice theory.
15 See Alves (2008).
16 Hayek (1998, Vol. 3, p. 203). In the same context Hayek stresses that: 'Long before Calvin the Italian and Dutch commercial towns had practised and later the Spanish schoolmen codified the rules which made the market economy possible.'

[17] In addition to Chafuen (2003), which is focused directly on the economic thought of the late scholastics, see for example Woods (2005), Booth (2007), and Gregg (2003 and 2007). In this context the notable work developed by the *Acton Institute for the Study of Religion and Liberty* should also be mentioned.

[18] See Chafuen (2003, p. 42).

[19] As noted by Biermann (1971, p. 479): 'Today, after the collapse of colonialism, the efforts of Las Casas to secure the Christianization of the Indians by peaceful, voluntary means represent an early, shining, though incomplete application of the principles that should govern missionary work among non-Christian peoples.'

[20] See Chapter 2 of this book.

[21] Quoted in Hamilton (1963, pp. 103–104).

[22] For a range of contemporary positions by libertarian authors on immigration, see for example Block (1998), Hoppe (1998), Huerta de Soto (1998) and Simon (1998).

[23] See for example Hamilton (1963, p. 150). The topic of just war is developed in Chapter 2 of this book.

[24] See Chapters 2 and 3 of this book and also Hamilton (1963, pp. 110–111).

[25] As noted by Reichberg et al. (2006, p. 98): 'The stark indictment of war for the sake of religion pronounced by early modern writers such as Gentili, Vitoria, and Suárez has been combined with a belief in human rights and territorial sovereignty to produce an all but unanimous conclusion among Christians that military crusades are military wrong. But in a world where a host of political leaders speak of intervening in other countries and regions to spread democratic values, the crusading spirit – albeit secularized – seems not to be so foreign after all. Furthermore, many modern Muslims hold that the concept of *jihad* (struggle) – while primarily meant to be spiritual, and if related to warfare, mainly defensive – can be used to legitimize religiously inspired struggles. To say that the idea of "holy wars" is dead, an artefact of the past, is thus more than dubious.'

[26] The importance of self-esteem and (ordered) self-interest as particularly relevant for the Jesuit scholastics. As pointed out by Höpfl (2004, p. 89), for the early Jesuit authors, 'the subjects' pre-eminent concern with their private good was not evidence of moral depravity' since 'to love oneself was a natural instinct implanted by God and even a duty.'

# Bibliography

Acton, John Emerich Edward Dalberg (1985), *Selected Writings of Lord Acton, Vol. I: Essays in the History of Liberty*. Indianapolis: Liberty Fund.
Afanasiev, Valeri L. (1971), 'The Literary Heritage of Bartolomé de Las Casas' in Juan Friede and Benjamin Keen (eds), *Bartlomé de Las Casas in History: Toward an Understanding of the Man and His Work*. DeKalb: Northern Illinois University Press, pp. 539–578.
Alves, André Azevedo (2006), *Ordem, Liberdade e Estado: Uma reflexão crítica sobre a filosofia política em Hayek e Buchanan*. Porto: Edições Praedicare.
—(2008), 'Economia de Mercado e Doutrina Social da Igreja' *Nova Cidadania* 35, 60–63.
Alves, André Azevedo and José Manuel Moreia (2009), 'Locke e a Escola de Salamanca' in Carlos Morujão e Luís Moia (eds) *John Locke nos 300 anos da sua morte*. Lisbon: Universidade Católica Portuguesa, pp. 165–179.
Aquinas, Thomas (1998), *Aquinas Selected Philosophical Writings*. Oxford: Oxford University Press.
—(2002), *Aquinas Political Writings* (edited by R. W. Dyson). Cambridge: Cambridge University Press.
Araujo, Enrique Diaz (1995), *Las Casas, Visto de Costado: Crítica bibliográfica sobre la Leyenda Negra*. Madrid: Fundación Francisco Elias de Tejada y Erasmo Pèrcopo.
Azpilcueta, Martín de (2007), 'Commentary on the Resolution of Money' (the original edition is from 1556) in Stephen J. Grabill (ed.) *Sourcebook in Late-Scholastic Monetary Theory*. Lanham: Lexington Books, pp. 18–107.
Bandelier, Adolph Francis (1908), 'Bartolomé de las Casas' *The Catholic Encyclopedia*. Vol. 3. New York: Robert Appleton Company [accessed on 29 Aug. 2008 from http://www.newadvent.org/cathen/03397a.htm].
Barry, Norman (2003), 'The Origins of Liberty and the Market: The Work of Marjorie-Grice Hutchinson (1909–2003)' *Economic Affairs* 23, 42–45.

Bataillon, Marcel (1971), 'The Clérigo Casas, Colonist and Colonial Reformer' in Juan Friede and Benjamin Keen (eds), *Bartlomé de las Casas in History: Toward an Understanding of the Man and His Work*. DeKalb: Northern Illinois University Press, pp. 353–440.

Belda Plans, Juan (2000), *La Escuela de Salamanca y la renovación de la teología en el siglo XVI*. Madrid: Biblioteca de Autores Cristianos.

Béltran, Lucas (1989), *Historia de las Doctrinas Económicas*. Barcelona: Teide.

—(1996), 'El Padre Juan de Mariana' in Lucas Beltrán, *Ensayos de Economia Política*. Madrid: Unión Editorial, pp. 255–266.

Biermann, Benno M. (1971), 'Bartolomé de Las Casas and Verapaz' in Juan Friede and Benjamin Keen (eds), *Bartlomé de las Casas in History: Toward an Understanding of the Man and His Work*. DeKalb: Northern Illinois University Press, pp. 237–484.

Block, Walter (1998), 'A Libertarian Case for Free Immigration' *Journal of Libertarian Studies* 13, (2), 167–186.

Booth, Philip (ed.) (2007), *Catholic Social Teaching and the Market Economy*. London: The Institute of Economic Affairs.

Braun, Harald E. (2007), *Juan de Mariana and Early Modern Spanish Political Thought*. Aldershot: Ashgate.

Brett, Annabel S. (1997), *Liberty, Right and Nature: Individual Rights in Later Scholastic Thought*. Cambridge: Cambridge University Press.

Burke, Peter (2006), 'Tacitism, Scepticism, and Reason of State' in J. H. Burns (with the assistance of Mark Goldie), *The Cambridge History of Political Thought 1450–1700*. Cambridge: Cambridge University Press, pp. 479–498.

Burns, J. H. (2006), 'Scholasticism: Survival and Revival' in J. H. Burns (with the assistance of Mark Goldie), *The Cambridge History of Political Thought 1450–1700*. Cambridge: Cambridge University Press, pp. 132–155.

Cajetan, Thomas de Vio Cardinal (2007), 'On Exchanging Money' (with an introduction by Raymond de Roover; the original edition is from 1499) *Journal of Markets & Morality* 10, (1), 193–252.

Camacho, Francisco Gómez (2007), 'Introduction to *Treatise on Money* (1597) by Luis e Molina, S. J.' in Stephen J. Grabill (ed.) *Sourcebook in Late-Scholastic Monetary Theory*. Lanham: Lexington Books, pp. 111–135.

Carro, Venancio D. (1968), 'Introducción General' in Domingo de Soto (1968). *De iustitia et iure*. Madrid: Instituto de Estúdios Políticos, pp. xiii–lxiv.

—(1971), 'The Spanish Theological-Juridical Renaissance and the Ideology of Bartolomé de Las Casas' in Juan Friede and Benjamin Keen (eds), *Bartlomé de las Casas in History: Toward an Understanding of the Man and His Work.* DeKalb: Northern Illinois University Press, pp. 237–277.

Castro, Daniel (2007), *Another Face of Empire: Bartolomé de Las Casas, Indigeneous Rights, and Ecclesiastical Imperialism.* Durham: Duke University Press.

Chafuen, Alejandro A. (2003), *Faith and Liberty: The Economic Thought of the Late Scholastics.* Lanham: Lexington Books.

—(2007), 'Introduction to *A Treatise on the Alteration of Money* (1609) by Juan de Mariana, S.J.' in Stephen J. Grabill (ed.), *Sourcebook in Late-Scholastic Monetary Theory.* Lanham: Lexington Books, pp. 241–245.

Comas, Juan (1971), 'Historical Reality and the Detractors of Father Las Casas' in Juan Friede and Benjamin Keen (eds), *Bartlomé de las Casas in History: Toward an Understanding of the Man and His Work.* DeKalb: Northern Illinois University Press, pp. 487–537.

Dyson, R. W. (2002), 'Introduction' in *Aquinas Political Writings* (edited by R. W. Dyson). Cambridge: Cambridge University Press, pp. xvii–xxxvi.

Ekelund, Robert B., Robert F. Hébert, and Robert D. Tollison (2006), *The Marketplace of Christianity.* Cambridge, MA: The MIT Press.

Fernandéz, Manuel Giménez (1971), 'Fray Bartolomé de Las Casas: A Biographical Sketch' in Juan Friede and Benjamin Keen (eds), *Bartlomé de las Casas in History: Toward an Understanding of the Man and His Work.* DeKalb: Northern Illinois University Press, pp. 67–125.

Fernandéz-Santamaria, J. A. (1977), *The State, War and Peace: Spanish Political Thought in the Renaissance 1516–1559.* Cambridge: Cambridge University Press.

Fortin, Ernest L. (1987), 'St. Thomas Aquinas' in Leo Strauss and Joseph Cropsey (eds) *History of Political Philosophy* (3rd edn). Chicago: The University of Chicago Press, pp. 248–275.

Freddoso, Alfred J. (1988), 'Introduction' in Molina (1988), *On Divine Foreknowledge: Part IV of the Concordia.* Ithaca: Cornell University Press.

Galindo García, Ángel (1999), 'El comercio con las Indias y su influencia en la expansión española. Breve reflexión desde el pensamiento de Tomás de Mercado', in *Europa, Mercado o Comunidad? De la Escuela de Salamaca a la Europa del Futuro.* Salamanca: Publicaciones Universidad Pontificia, pp. 53–78.

Gierke, Otto (1957), *Natural Law and the Theory of Society 1500 to 1800* (translated and with an introduction by Ernest Baker, first published in 1934). Boston: Beacon Press.

—(1987), *Political Theories of the Middle Age* (translated and with an introduction by F. W. Maitland, first published in 1900). Cambridge: Cambridge University Press.

Gordley, James (1991), *The Philosophical Origins of Modern Contract Doctrine*. Oxford: Clarendon Press.
—(2006), *Foundations of Private Law: Property, Tort, Contract, Unjust Enrichment*. Oxford: Oxford University Press.
Grabill, Stephen J. (2007), 'Editor's Introduction' in Stephen J. Grabill (ed.) *Sourcebook in Late-Scholastic Monetary Theory*. Lanham: Lexington Books, pp. xiii–xxxv.
Gregg, Samuel (2003), *On Ordered Liberty: A Treatise on the Free Society (Religion, Politics, and Society in the New Millennium)*. Lanham: Lexington Books.
—(2007), *The Commercial Society: Foundations and Challenges in a Global Age*. Lanham: Lexington Books.
—(2008), 'Natural law, Scholasticism and free markets' in Stephen F. Copp (ed.), *The Legal Foundations of Free Markets*. London: The Institute of Economic Affairs, pp. 65–83.
Grice-Hutchinson, Marjorie (1952), *The School of Salamanca: Readings in Spanish Monetary Theory 1544–1605*. Oxford: Clarendon Press.
—(1978), *Early Economic Thought in Spain 1177–1740*. London: George Allen & Unwin.
—(1993), 'The Concept of the School of Salamanca: Its Origins and Development' in Laurence S. Moss and Christopher K. Ryan (eds) *Economic Thought in Spain: Selected Essays of Marjorie Grice-Hutchinson*. Aldershot: Edward Elgar, pp. 23–29 (originally published in 1989 as 'El concepto de la Escuela de Salamanca: sus origins y desarollo' in *Revista de Historia Económica*, VII (2), supplement, Madrid: Primavera-Verano).
Haldane, John (2004), *Faithful Reason: Essays Catholic and Philosophical*. London: Routledge.
Hamilton, Bernice (1963), *Political Thought in Sixteenth-Century Spain: A Study of the Political Ideas of Vitoria, Soto, Suárez, and Molina*. Oxford: Oxford University Press.
Hanke, Lewis (1994), *All Mankind is One: A Study of the Disputation between Bartlomé de Las Casas and Juan Ginés de Sepúlveda in 1550 on the Intellectual and Religious Capacity of the American Indians*. DeKalb: Northern Illinois University Press.
—(2002), *The Spanish Struggle for Justice in the Conquest of America* (with previously unpublished personal and professional reminiscence by the author and an Introduction by Susan Scafidi and Peter Bakewell). Dallas: Southern Methodist University Press.
Hayek, Friedrich A. (1974), 'Lecture to the Memory of Alfred Nobel, December 11, 1974' in Assar Lindbeck (ed.) (1992), *Nobel Lectures, Economics 1969–1980*. Singapore: World Scientific Publishing Co. [accessed on 16 Aug. 2008 from http://nobelprize.org/economics/laureates/1974/hayek-lecture.html].

—(1998), *Law, Legislation and Liberty: A New Statement of the Liberal Principles of Justice and Political Economy*. London: Routledge.
Höpfl, Harro (2004), *Jesuit Political Thought: The Society of Jesus and the State, c. 1540–1630*. Cambridge: Cambridge University Press.
Hoppe, Hans-Hermann (1998), 'The Case for Free Trade and Restricted Immigration' *Journal of Libertarian Studies* 13, (2), 221–233.
Huerta de Soto, Jesús (1996), 'New Light on the Prehistory of the Theory of Banking and the School of Salamanca' *Review of Austrian Economics* 9, (2), 59–81.
—(1998), 'A Libertarian Theory of Free Immigration' *Journal of Libertarian Studies* 13, (2), 187–197.
—(1999) 'Juan de Mariana and the Spanish Scholastics' in Randall G. Holcombe (ed.) (1999), *Fifteen Great Austrian Economists*. Auburn, Alabama: Ludwig von Mises Institute.
—(2006), *Money, Bank Credit, and Economic Cycles* (translated by Melinda A. Stroup). Auburn, Alabama: Ludwig von Mises Institute.
John Paul II (1991), *Centesimus Annus* [accessed on 12 Mar. 2009 from http://www.vatican.va/holy_father/john_paul_ii/encyclicals/documents/hf_jp-ii_enc_01051991_centesimus-annus_en.html].
Juana, Rodrigo Muñoz (2007), 'Introduction to Commentary on the Resolution of Money (1556) by Martín de Azpilcueta' in Stephen J. Grabill (ed.) *Sourcebook in Late-Scholastic Monetary Theory*. Lanham: Lexington Books, pp. 3–15.
Kenny, Anthony (1979), *The God of the Philosophers*. Oxford: Oxford University Press.
Kingdon, Robert M. (2006), 'Calvinism and resistance theory, 1550–1580' in J. H. Burns (with the assistance of Mark Goldie), *The Cambridge History of Political Thought 1450–1700*. Cambridge: Cambridge University Press, pp. 193–218.
Las Casas, Bartolomé de (1971), *Bartolomé de Las Casas: A Selection of His Writings* (translated and edited by George Sanderlin). New York: Alfred A. Knopf.
—(1992 [ca. 1552]), *In Defense of the Indians: The Defense of the Most Reverend Lord, Don Fray Bartolomé De Las Casas, of the Order of Preachers, Late Bishop of Chiapa, against the Persecutors and Slanderers of the Peoples of the New World Discovered across the Seas* (translated by Stafford Poole and with a Foreword by Martin E. Marty). DeKalb: Northern Illinois University Press.
—(2004 [ca. 1552]), *A Short Account of the Destruction of the Indies* (translated by Nigel Griffin and with an Introduction by Anthony Pagden). London: Penguin Books.
Lehmkuhl, Augustinus (1910), 'Juan Mariana' *The Catholic Encyclopedia*. Vol. 9. New York: Robert Appleton Company [accessed on 12 Aug. 2008 from http://www.newadvent.org/cathen/09659b.htm].

Lloyd, Howell A. (2006), 'Constitutionalism' in J. H. Burns (with the assistance of Mark Goldie), *The Cambridge History of Political Thought 1450–1700*. Cambridge: Cambridge University Press, pp. 254–297.

Locke, John (1990 [1689]), *A Letter Concerning Toleration*. New York: Prometheus Books.

Losada, Ángel (1971), 'The Controversy between Sepúlveda and Las Casas in the Junta of Valladolid' in Juan Friede and Benjamin Keen (eds), *Bartlomé de las Casas in History: Toward an Understanding of the Man and His Work*. DeKalb: Northern Illinois University Press, pp. 279–306.

Loyola, Ignatius of (1989), *The Spiritual Exercises of Saint Ignatius: St. Ignatius Profound Precepts of Mystical Theology* (translated by Anthony Mottola and with an Introduction by Robert W. Gleason; since the original draft by Ignatius has been lost, the translation is from the oldest – 1541 – text in existence in conjunction with the 1920 Latin text *Exercitia Spiritualia Sancti Patris Ignatii de Loyola*, by John Roothaan). New York: Image Books/Doubleday.

Marcus, Raymond (1971), 'Las Casas in Literature' in Juan Friede and Benjamin Keen (eds), *Bartlomé de las Casas in History: Toward an Understanding of the Man and His Work*. DeKalb: Northern Illinois University Press, pp. 581–600.

Mariana, Juan de (2007), 'Treatise on the Alteration of Money' (the original edition is from 1609) in Stephen J. Grabill (ed.) *Sourcebook in Late-Scholastic Monetary Theory*. Lanham: Lexington Books, pp. 247–341.

McDermott, Timothy (1998), 'Introduction', in *Aquinas Selected Philosophical Writings* (edited by Timothy McDermott). Oxford: Oxford University Press, pp. xi–xxxii.

Meadowcroft, John (2005), *The Ethics of the Market*. Basingstoke: Palgrave Macmillian.

Melé, Domènec (1999), 'Early Business Ethics in Spain: The Salamanca School (1526–1614)' *Journal of Business Ethics* 22, 175–189.

Melody, John (1908) 'Diego Covarruvias' in *The Catholic Encyclopedia*. Vol. 4. New York: Robert Appleton Company. [accessed on 16 Apr. 2009 from http://www.newadvent.org/cathen/04457a.htm].

Mercado, Tomás de (1975), *Suma de tratos y contratos*, with an introductory study by R. Sierra Bravo. Madrid: Editora Nacional.

Molina, Luís de (1981), *La Teoría del Justo Precio*. Madrid: Editora Nacional.

—(1988), *On Divine Foreknowledge: Part IV of the Concordia* (translated and with an Introduction and notes by Alfred J. Freddoso; the first edition of Molina's *Concordia* is from 1588). Ithaca: Cornell University Press.

## Bibliography

Montes, Javier Alejo (1998), *La Universidad de Salamanca Bajo Filipe II, 1575–1598*. Burgos: Junta de Castilla y León.
Moreira, José Manuel (1992), 'Luis de Molina e as origens ibéricas da economia de mercado' in *Actas do Encontro Ibérico sobre História do Pensamento Económico*. Lisboa: CISEP, pp. 41–62.
—(1996), *Ética, Economia e Política*. Porto: Lello Editores.
—(1999), *A Contas com a Ética Empresarial*. Cascais: Principia.
Oakley, Francis (2006), 'Christian obedience and authority, 1520–1550' in J. H. Burns (with the assistance of Mark Goldie), *The Cambridge History of Political Thought 1450–1700*. Cambridge: Cambridge University Press, pp. 159–192.
Ozment, Steven (1980), *The Age of Reform, 1250–1550: An Intellectual and Religious History of Late Medieval and Reformation Europe*. New Haven: Yale University Press.
Pagden, Anthony (2002), *Peoples and Empires: Europeans and the Rest of the World, from Antiquity to the Present*. London: Phoenix Press.
—(2004), 'Introduction' in Casas, Bartolomé de Las (2004 [ca. 1552]), *A Short Account of the Destruction of the Indies*. London: Penguin Books, pp. xiii–xli.
Pagden, Anthony and Jeremy Lawrence (1991), 'Introduction' in Anthony Pagden and Jeremy Lawrence (ed.), *Vitoria: Political Writings* (Cambridge Texts in the History of Political Thought). Cambridge: Cambridge University Press.
Pereña Vicente, Luciano (1957), *Diego de Covarrubias y Leyva, Maestro de Derecho Internacional*. Madrid: Asociación Francisco de Vitoria.
Pérez Goyena, António (1912), 'Francisco Suárez' *The Catholic Encyclopedia*. Vol. 14. New York: Robert Appleton Company. [accessed on 11 Aug. 2008 from http://www.newadvent.org/cathen/14319a.htm].
Pohle, Joseph (1911), 'Luis de Molina' in *The Catholic Encyclopedia*. Vol. 10. New York: Robert Appleton Company. [accessed on 10 Aug. 2008 from http://www.newadvent.org/cathen/10436a.htm].
Pribram, Karl (1983), *A History of Economic Reasoning*. Baltimore: The Johns Hopkins University Press.
Reichberg, Gregory, Henrik Syse and Endre Begby (eds) (2006), *The Ethics of War: Classic and Contemporary Readings*. Malden: Blackwell Publishing.
Rivas, León Gómez (1999), 'Business Ethics and The History of Economics in Spain. "The School of Salamanca: A Bibliography"' *Journal of Business Ethics* 22, 191–202.
Rizo Patrón, Francisco (2006), 'El Pensamiento Juridico de la Escuela de Salamanca, Concreción de la Ley Natural en la Configuración de la Cultura' paper from the *II Jornadas Internacionales de Derecho Natural* – Pontificia Universidad Católica Argentina.

Rommen, Heinrich A. (1945), *The State in Catholic Thought: A Treatise in Political Philosophy*. St Louis: B. Herder Book Co.
—(1948), 'Francis Suarez' *The Review of Politics* 10, (4), 437–461.
Roover, Raymond de (1955), 'Scholastic Economics: Survival and Lasting Influence from the Sixteenth Century to Adam Smith' *The Quarterly Journal of Economics* 69, (2), 161–190.
—(1958), 'The Concept of the Just Price: Theory and Economic Policy' *The Journal of Economic History* 18, (4), 418–434.
Rothbard, Murray N. (2006), *Economic Thought before Adam Smith (An Austrian Perspective on the History of Economic Thought: Vol. I)*. Auburn: Ludwig von Mises Institute.
Sally, Razeen (2008), *New Frontiers in Free Trade: Globalization's Future and Asia's Rising Role*. Washington, DC: Cato Institute.
Salmon, J. H. M. (2006), 'Catholic Resistance Theory, Ultramontanism, and the Royalist Response, 1580–1620' in J. H. Burns (with the assistance of Mark Goldie), *The Cambridge History of Political Thought 1450–1700*. Cambridge: Cambridge University Press, pp. 219–253.
Saranyana, Josep-Ignasi (2007), *La Filosofía Medieval*. Navarrra: Ediciones Universidade de Navarra.
Schumpeter, Joseph A. (1994), *History of Economic Analysis* (ed. Elisabeth Boody Schumpeter). London: Routledge.
Scott, James Brown (1934), *The Spanish Origin of International Law: Francisco De Vitoria and His Law of Nations*. London: Humphrey Milford (there is a 2000 reprint by The Lawbook Exchange).
Simon, Julian L. (1998), 'Are There Grounds for Limiting Immigration?' *Journal of Libertarian Studies* 13, (2), 137–152.
Skinner, Quentin (1978), *The Foundations of Modern Political Thought – Vol. 2: The Age of Reformation*. Cambridge: Cambridge University Press.
Soto, Domingo de (1968), *De iustitia et iure* (facsimile of the 1556 Latin edition accompanied with a Spanish translation). Madrid: Instituto de Estúdios Políticos.
Termes, Rafael (1999), 'Humanismo y ética para el mercado europeo', in *Europa, Mercado o Comunidad? De la Escuela de Salamaca a la Europa del Futuro*. Salamanca: Publicaciones Universidad Pontificia, pp. 25–40.
Vitoria, Francisco de (1991), *Vitoria: Political Writings* (edited by Anthony Pagden and Jeremy Lawrence, Cambridge Texts in the History of Political Thought). Cambridge: Cambridge University Press.
Watner, Carl (1987), '"All Mankind Is One": The Libertarian Tradition in Sixteenth Century Spain' *The Journal of Libertarian Studies* 8, (2), 293–309.
Wood, Diana (2002), *Medieval Economic Thought*. Cambridge: Cambridge University Press.

Woods, Thomas E. Jr. (2005), *The Church and the Market: A Catholic Defense of the Free Economy*. Lanham: Lexington Books.

Zaratiegui, Jesús M. (2000), 'La propiedad en algunos autores de la escuela de Salamanca', *Cuadernos de Ciencias Económicas y Empresariales*, 37, 87–93.

# Index

absolutism  45, 49–51, 103–4, 127, 134
  *see also* divine right of kings; political power; resistance theory
Alcalá, University of  3, 9, 14, 19, 20, 22, 23, 30, 121, 136
Aquinas, St. Thomas  3, 4, 13, 14, 20, 24–34, 70, 74, 124, 127, 130, 131
Aristotle  3, 24, 26–7, 34, 62, 66, 72, 101, 135
Augustine, St.  37
Azpilcueta, Martín de  15–16, 44, 106
  banking  77–8
  extreme need  70
  price controls  73
  quantity theory of money  79–80

banking, theories of  76–8
  *see also* inflation; quantity theory of money
Bonacina, Martino  106
Buchanan, James  111, 136
business *see* commerce; trade

Cajetan, Cardinal Thomas de Vio  30, 57, 74, 79, 131
Cano, Melchor  98
Carranza, Bartolomé de  98
Catholic social thought  115–17
Church and state  25, 55–9
  *see also* political power

Coimbra, University of  2, 3, 15, 19, 22, 135
commerce  17–18, 60, 65–71
  weights, measurements and money  81–3
common good  17, 28, 32–4, 39, 46–7, 51, 55, 65–7, 70–1, 73, 84–5, 103, 110, 120
  individual rights  39–45
conservatism  4–5, 13, 39–40, 111, 115, 118, 119–20, 137
constitutionalism  45, 86, 127, 135
Counter-Reformation, Catholic  9, 12, 34–9, 102–3
Covarrubias y Leyva, Diego de  16–17, 87, 108, 122–3
  Just War theory  61–2
  individual rights  44–5
  monetary theory  79
  Sepúlveda  98
  slavery and the *ius gentium*  129
  value theory  72
Crockaert, Pierre  13, 30

*damnum emergens*  75
  *see also* interest; usury
Diana, Antonino  106
divine right of kings  103–4
  *see also* absolutism; political power; resistance theory
division of labour  69

Escobar, Antonio de  106
*encomienda*  18–19, 90–5, 123
Évora, University of  2, 3, 19, 135

Eximius, Doctor *see* Suárez, Francisco
extreme need  69–71, 117

Fonseca, Pedro de  106, 135
fractional-reserve banking *see* banking, theories of

Galiani, Ferdinando  108
Gregory XIII, Pope  16
Grotius, Hugo  105–6, 108, 128
Guatemala  19, 124

Hayek, Friedrich  1, 111, 112, 114, 115, 136, 137
Heidegger, Martin  111
Hobbes, Thomas  104, 107, 126
Hutcheson, Francis  108, 136

Ignatius of Loyola  37–8
  *see also* Society of Jesus
immigration  118, 138
individual rights  4, 32–3, 39–45, 53, 65, 86, 87, 99, 110, 117, 120, 125, 126
inflation  11, 79–83
interest  73–6, 77, 113, 131
  *see also* usury; banking, theories of
international law  1, 4, 14, 15, 16, 22, 59–61, 86, 87, 99, 105, 128, 129
  *see also* Just War theory
international trade  69, 118
  *see also* commerce; trade
*ius gentium*  59–61, 67, 112
  *see also* international law

John Paul II, Pope  116
just price  71–3
  *see also* commerce; inflation; price theory; value theory

Just War theory  4, 61–5, 97, 105, 129
  and the colonization of America  95–100
  *see also ius gentium*, international law

Las Casas, Bartolomé de  18–19, 87
  disputation with Sepúlveda  95–100
  legacy  100–2
  social experiments in America  90–5
law
  divine  27, 29–30, 58
  eternal  27
  human  27–30, 45–8, 72, 112, 124
  international *see* international law
  of nations *see* international law; *ius gentium*
  natural *see* natural law theory
  positive  32–3, 40, 43, 46, 49
Laws of Burgos  89, 92
legal price  72–3
  *see also* commerce; inflation; price theory; value theory
legitimate resistance
  *see* resistance theory
Leo X  75
Lessius, Leonard  22, 106, 135
libertarianism  4, 5, 13, 21, 40, 111, 115, 118–20, 123
Locke, John  55, 107–8, 126, 127–8, 135–6
Lombard, Peter  3, 26, 30–1
*lucrum cessans*  75
  *see also* interest; usury
Lugo, Juan de  2, 131, 135, 137
Luther, Martin  35–8, 134–5

## Index

Mariana, Juan de  20–2, 37, 123, 126, 137
  common good  43
  currency debasement and inflation  82–3, 132
  division of labour  69
  money and commerce  82
  political power  58, 135
  price controls  73
  public expenditure and taxation  85
  tyrannicide  44, 53–5, 127
Mercado, Tomás de  17–18
  money  81
  private property and self-interest  68
Mises, Ludwig von  131, 137
Molina, Luis de  2, 19–20, 22, 27, 37, 87, 105, 106, 111, 113, 135, 136
  banking  77
  common good  43, 85
  international trade and immigration  59–60, 118
  *ius gentium*  59
  monetary theory  80
  political power  49
  price theory  72–3
  self-defense  43
  taxation  85
monetary theory  79–83
Montesinos, Antonio de  18, 87–90, 91, 102

natural law theory  2, 4, 24, 39, 58, 60, 61, 65, 89, 105, 106, 110, 113–14, 120
  individual rights  39–45
  political power  46–52
  property  66–7
  Thomist  25–35, 104
  universality  96

Navarrus, Doctor *see* Azpilcueta, Martín de
New Laws of 1542  19, 90, 95–6
nominalism  14, 30–1, 124

original condition  41, 47–50
  *see also* individual rights; political power; state of nature

parental rights  56
  *see also* individual rights
Paris, University of  13, 14, 20, 26, 30
Paul III, Pope  9, 38, 93
Peru  109
Pius V, Pope  16, 123
*poena conventionalis*  75
  *see also* interest; usury
political power  41, 43–51, 53, 58, 103–4, 126–7, 135
  *see also* absolutism, common good; constitutionalism
  individual rights; resistance theory
Portugal  2, 3, 6–7, 10–11, 19, 83, 97–8, 106, 112, 135
price controls  73, 131
price theory  71–3, 80–2, 113
  *see also* commerce; inflation; value theory
private property  43–4, 50, 59, 61, 65–9, 93–4, 96, 113, 116–17, 118–19, 126, 129, 130
  self-interest  73
Protestantism *see* Reformation, Protestant
public finance  83–5
  *see also* inflation
Pufendorf, Samuel von  104, 106, 108

quantity theory of money 21, 23, 97–103

Rand, Ayn 137
Reformation, Protestant 9, 12, 24, 35–8, 56, 103
resistance theory 34, 45, 46, 51–5, 58, 104, 119, 135
  *see also* tyrannicide
Rothbard, Murray N. 12, 26, 76, 108, 131, 135, 137

Salamanca, University of 1, 2, 8, 10–11, 13, 15, 17, 18, 22, 31, 87, 109
Salamanca School
  applied political thought 39–65
  contemporary relevance 110–20
  decline 11–12
  economic thought 65–85
  influence on subsequent authors 105–9
  key authors 13–23
  New World (America) 86–102
  philosophical and political foundations 24–34
  political and intellectual context 6–11
  theological-political impact 102–4
San Marcos, University of 109, 136
Schopenhauer, Arthur 111
self-defence 42–4, 50–1, 61–2, 119, 129, 133
  *see also* individual rights, Just War theory
Sepúlveda, Juan Ginés 19, 90
  disputation with Las Casas 95–100

Sixtus V, Pope 16
Smith, Adam 108, 136
social experiments in America 90–5
  *see also* Las Casas, Bartolomé de
Society of Jesus 9, 19, 20, 22, 25, 37–8, 134
Soto, Domingo de 14–15, 16, 19, 27, 31, 87, 106, 109, 122, 125, 126, 129, 130
  banking 77
  civil power and spiritual power 58
  disputation between Las Casas and Sepúlveda 98–100
  *ius gentium* 59, 67
  natural law and natural right 42–3
  private property 67–8
  taxation 84–5
Spain 1–11, 11–12, 13–23, 72, 79, 80–1, 83, 124
  New World (America) 86–102, 133
Spiritual Exercises 37, 125
spiritual power and civil power 58–9
  *see also* Church and state; political power
state of nature 47–8, 67
  *see also* individual rights; original condition; political power
Suárez, Francisco 2, 22–3, 27, 31–2, 37, 57, 87, 103–6, 111, 118, 125, 126, 127, 129, 132, 135, 138
  common good 43
  *ius gentium* 59–61, 112, 137
  political power 49–51
  resistance 52–3

taxation 82, 83–5
  *see also* inflation
Thomism
  European revival of 3–5,
    13–14, 24, 30–4
  natural law 25–30
Tordesillas, Treaty of 6
trade 17–18, 60, 65–71
  *see also* international trade;
    private property
Trent, Council of 9, 14–15, 16,
  20, 36–7, 102, 105, 121–2
tyrannicide 45, 51–5
  *see also* constitutionalism;
    Mariana, Juan; political
    power; resistance theory

usury 16, 71, 73–6, 106,
  113, 131
  *see also* interest; banking,
    theories of

value theory 17, 71–3, 79–81,
  108, 113
  *see also* monetary theory; price
    theory
Vázquez de Menchaca,
  Fernando 105–6
Vico, Gian Battista 111

war *see* Just War theory
Weber, Max 115
Woff, Christian 111

www.ingramcontent.com/pod-product-compliance
Lightning Source LLC
Chambersburg PA
CBHW061840300426
44115CB00013B/2460